MILLION DOLLAR ARM

MILLION DOLLAR ARM

Sometimes to Win, You Have to Change the Game

J. B. BERNSTEIN

with Rebecca Paley

**SIMON &
SCHUSTER**

London · New York · Sydney · Toronto · New Delhi

A CBS COMPANY

First published in Great Britain by Simon & Schuster UK Ltd, 2014
A CBS COMPANY

3 5 7 9 10 8 6 4 2

Simon & Schuster UK Ltd
1st Floor
222 Gray's Inn Road
London WC1X 8HB

www.simonandschuster.co.uk

Simon & Schuster Australia, Sydney
Simon & Schuster India, New Delhi

Cover photograph © 2014 Disney

A CIP catalogue record for this book
is available from the British Library

ISBN: 978-1-47113-622-1
Ebook ISBN: 978-47113-623-8

Interior design by Julie Schroeder
Printed and bound by CPI Group (UK) Ltd, Croydon, CR0 4YY

Insert photograph credits: pages 1-4: Seven Figures Management, LLC; page 5:
top and middle by Seven Figures Management, LLC, bottom by Lisa LaFon/
Seven Figures Management, LLC; page 6: top and middle © 2014 Disney, bottom
by Seven Figures Management, LLC; page 7, from top to bottom: Seven Figures
Management, LLC, Mark Ciardi/Seven Figures Management, LLC, © 2014 Disney,
the Bernstein family; page 8: top by Seven Figures Management, LLC,
middle and bottom by J.B.Bernstein/Seven Figures Management, LLC

PROLOGUE

Their crisp white *Million Dollar Arm* uniforms gleaming in the bright Arizona sun, Rinku and Dinesh took the field. They had spent the last hour warming up inside the training facility, throwing 90-mile-per-hour fastballs that hit the catcher's mitt with lots of mustard and a satisfying pop. They were locked in and ready to go. About to face a crowd of pro scouts, the two were far from finished projects, but to look at them, you'd never guess that just a year before, they had never touched a baseball. Hell, a year ago, they didn't even know what a baseball was.

These two guys, who hailed from the kind of small, rural Indian villages where many people didn't have indoor plumbing, running electricity, or opportunities for work, found themselves in Tempe that early-November morning to compete for a spot in the bigs. The experiment began a year earlier with a zany idea to canvass India, where baseball is virtually unknown, in search of raw pitching talent. Rinku and Dinesh were the winners of the nationwide contest and reality TV show. Now they were trying to make history as the first natives of India to become pro athletes in the United States.

The training facility where we were holding the tryout, housed in an ordinary office park adjacent to a strip mall, didn't exactly look like the stuff of Cooperstown. But it was one of the top facilities in Arizona. Several office suites had been combined to create a beautiful, modern space with cold tubs for ice baths, workout equipment, an indoor pitching mound, and the like. Out the back door and across a parking lot was a strip of Astroturf with a pitching mound and pitching cage specifically designed for pitchers and hitters to train.

Behind home plate stood thirty stony-faced scouts. It was unbelievable, even surreal, how many scouts had turned out to see if Rinku and Dinesh could throw. These travel-hardened vets of the sport, who will look under any and every rock for the next megastar, couldn't stay away from our tryout, no matter how ridiculous a long shot it was.

The scouts weren't the only ones eager to discover whether baseball can be learned well enough in a year to play in the pros. A huge crowd of media—including ESPN, *USA Today,* and local reporters and TV crews—had assembled, which was very atypical. No one ever covers baseball tryouts. Even a crazy, once-in-a-generation high school recruit is a tough sell to an editor. But two guys who, if they didn't do the impossible and land a spot on a baseball team, would be sent back to a life of hardship, at least by American standards? Well, *that* was newsworthy. Rinku's and Dinesh's tryout had all the melodrama and nail-biting potential heartbreak that make for an irresistible sports story.

When the time came to bring out Rinku and Dinesh, their pitching had been great, which wasn't always the case. While both had big-league potential, their lightning-quick education meant that their deliveries could be erratic. Some days were good, some days not so much. We wanted them to warm up inside so that they would come out looking sharp. And, thank God, today their mechanics were laser-focused.

When Rinku; Dinesh; their pitching coach, Tom House; talent scout and trainer Ray Poitevint; my business partners Ash Vasudevan and Will Chang; and I walked out of the building in one badass line, it was like a scene from *Reservoir Dogs*. (Well, maybe more like the scene from *Swingers* where they imitate *Reservoir Dogs*.) As Coach House started to introduce the boys, smiling and thanking everyone for coming out to see this miracle of baseball, our mini-entourage was buzzing with nerves. I was so pumped; I couldn't wait for them to get out on the mound. There wasn't a doubt in my mind that Rinku and Dinesh were going to nail this thing.

Dinesh was up first. The scouts, three deep, jostled one another and shoved their radar guns into place. (Scouts all bring their own guns, since they don't trust anyone.) Dozens of barrels pointed at Dinesh as he trotted out to the mound.

I'd never been more excited about anything in my life—and as a pro sports agent who had been in the business for more than twenty years, it took a lot to get me excited. I had seen and done just about everything: driven expensive cars, flown on private jets, partied at the hottest nightclubs, dated the prettiest girls, and watched the Super Bowl from the sidelines. But this was different. If Rinku and Dinesh showed the scouts the best they could do, it would change the courses of their lives and their families' lives forever. It would also vindicate me after most of the sports community told me I was an idiot when I first came up with the idea.

I felt great. Success was assured. There wasn't a hint that anything could go wrong—until someone pulled back the tarp that had been covering the mound. Suddenly, like a train wreck unfurling in slow motion, the entire situation went south. The mound, sandy, crumbling, and uneven, was totally messed up.

"Coach, mound no good," Dinesh said.

The scouts, their guns raised in the air, waited. There was no time.

"You gotta go," Coach House whispered loudly. "Just go!"

And just like when the guys left their villages back in India for a foreign land and a crazy dream, Dinesh took a major-league leap of faith, stepped up to the mound, and wound up for his first pitch.

CHAPTER 1

"J.B., man, you got to figure out a way to get me outta here."

The television commercial that was supposed to only take six hours was already veering north of eight, and my client, a sports superstar, was starting to lose it. I knew how this was going to go in the first hour of the LA shoot, when the director dragged out the schedule as if he were Martin Scorsese, so that by lunchtime, the line producer was already hinting that they might need my client for another half hour or so. The half hour came and went, and now my client was mad at me: he wanted *me* to call it a day. But what was I going to do? Pull the plug on a half-finished commercial? Even if that were doable, I couldn't afford to ruin my relationship with the massive sports marketing conglomerate over an extra hour of my client's time. And I couldn't make my client look like a bad guy who was sick of participating in this big payday.

So I started doing what I do best: spinning. I had to take the player's mind off the clock. First stop, the makeup truck. Makeup girls are always super-nice and have great stories about other celebrities. We killed a half hour listening to them dish on a big athlete who wouldn't let them put powder on his face. While the girls were talking, I had Mexican food from a great restaurant I knew in LA delivered to the set. He loved Mexican and couldn't get this kind of quality back home, so that provided another short diversion. Then I used my fail-proof method of discussing future business deals that would involve this athlete. I was like the storyteller in *One Thousand and One Nights,* improvising contractual issues and talking strategy until the director finally said it was a wrap, sparing my professional life.

I was still spinning in the car on my way back to the airport—but not to my client, who was already on his way to another part of the country. I pounded the cell phone, chasing deals. I heard that Gillette was looking for a name athlete to star in an ad campaign for a new razor and was pushing my way in to pitch. I called a stadium merchandiser to check up on the availability of one of my client's shirts.

The door of the airplane back to San Francisco closed, and the announcement was made to shut off all electronic devices, when my cell rang. I answered it; I always answer the phone. It was an exec I had been trying to reach for a month finally getting back to me. It was too late to get off the plane, so I started talking. Fast.

"Sir, please turn off your cell," the flight attendant said.

I held up my finger and got right to the point with the exec.

"Sir."

I didn't give the exec time to respond, since I wouldn't have time to respond to his response, but instead quickly segued into setting up a meeting with his secretary to talk more.

"Sir!"

He said yes—all I needed; all I ever needed—and I hung up right before air marshals came to escort me off the plane.

After touching down in San Francisco, I headed straight home to my 2,500-square-foot loft with thirty-foot floor-to-ceiling windows that overlooked the ballpark, only three blocks away. That's where I was headed that evening. I had to dress quickly in order to get to the stadium three hours before the Giants game for the necessary schmooze time. I changed into a long-sleeved V-neck Armani shirt, Ralph Lauren Black Label jeans, and a Gucci belt before opening up the box where I kept my watch collection. Each of the thirty timepieces, lined up as neatly as soldiers, represented a big milestone in my career. I had bought the Patek Philippe, Rolex, Audemars Piguet, and Breitling with parts of commissions I had earned—the reward I gave myself for doing well. I strapped on my Vacheron Constantin skeleton watch, its delicate wheels and gears exposed in a face devoid of any plate or bridges. That was the reward for the trading card deal I did with Barry Bonds, the largest ever for a player at the time. It was made possible because I was the only agent in the history of Major League Baseball to take a client out of the MLB Players Association group licensing agreement. I dropped *a lot* on that watch.

I left the car in my garage and opted to walk to the stadium in the cool late-afternoon air. Back when I lived in San Diego and LA in the midnineties, I had been a car fanatic who thought nothing of shelling out $700 a month in gas to run a sweet '63 Corvette convertible. Since then, I had lost the bug and was now satisfied with a souped-up Mustang convertible.

With a badge that gave me access to almost anywhere in AT&T Park, I started by paying a visit to the Giants players and coaches during warm-ups. After some chit-chat, I went over to the opposing team while it took batting practice in the cage. Then it was over to the zone where the media congregate. I kidded around with other agents and their players. Once the field cleared before the game started, I went to the underbelly of the stadium to schmooze with the people who ran the stadium merchandise, food, and beverage sales. Then it was up to work the rooms of the luxury suites that housed sponsors. As an agent, I always had to be in the mix.

Baseball is a long season, and even the most diehard fans don't stay to the bitter end of every game. Antsy by the seventh inning, I went down to the tunnel that connects the dugouts to the locker rooms, where girls hang out hoping to meet athletes. By now the night had turned from professional to personal. AT&T Park gets pretty cold no matter the time of year, so any girl dolled up in a miniskirt or other outfit that showed a lot of skin was clearly not there for the game. I approached a petite brunette in a tank top, short shorts, and heels: "My name is J.B. What's yours?"

I could tell in three seconds if a girl was interested. If she didn't make eye contact but instead continued to look around the room while I talked, then it was a no. Unlike guys who have to steel themselves to go up to a girl and then feel suicidal if rejected, "No" didn't affect me too much. It was just, who's next?

The brunette kept her eyes on mine while telling me her name. After a minute of small talk, she lightly brushed her hand against my shoulder as she laughed, signaling that the door was wide open. We were back at my place within a half hour. I hadn't even bought her a drink.

By two in the morning, unable to lie in bed anymore, I went to the living room and flipped on ESPN's *SportsCenter*. The brunette found me with my head in my laptop, firing off work emails.

"Do you want me out of here?" she asked.

"No. Why?"

"You seem restless."

"I'm just not tired."

I called her a cab, and she took off. I didn't care who was sleeping in my bed; business came first. If I was a jerk, then being a jerk was my dream.

There are two kinds of sports agents: those who handle the playing contracts with an athlete's team, and the marketing agents who handle everything else. There was never any question about which kind of agent I wanted to be. I saw playing contracts as a game of diminishing returns. The playing contract is earned by the player, who with time naturally becomes less and less valuable. But with marketing, there was no limit to how much off-field revenue I could generate for a guy through endorsements, TV commercials, personal appearances, memorabilia sales, and licensing everything from mugs to video games. It was on me alone to make the deals, and I took pride in creating those opportunities.

I worked at the Upper Deck Company, one of the biggest trading card and sports memorabilia companies, for about four years. I started as a manager of business development and then was the director of marketing and product development for Upper Deck Authenticated, their memorabilia subsidiary. So in 1994, after I left Upper

Deck and was working as an independent sports consultant to Major League Soccer in creating its licensing program for the teams and players, I got a call from Barry Sanders of the Detroit Lions. In my opinion, he is the best running back ever to play pro football (despite his being only third on the career yardage list), and he asked me if I would help him with his marketing. That call inspired me to take the plunge and start my own sports marketing company. Twelve years later, in a business I built from the ground up, I represented all Hall of Famers. In addition to Barry Sanders, there was Dallas Cowboys halfback Emmitt Smith, the number one running back on the career yardage list, and Curtis Martin of the New England Patriots and then the New York Jets, who is number four. (The second best in NFL history, the Chicago Bears' Walter Payton, was nearly retired when I started my career.) I also represented the Giants' Barry Bonds, who I believe is the greatest baseball player of all time.

My roster set me apart from other boutique agents, who typically work either with a bunch of small clients or one big client. It was rare to find a boutique business like mine, where all four clients are among the greatest that ever played. And I knew exactly to what I could credit my success: it wasn't that I was smarter or more connected than the other guys; it was that I took business seriously.

When I was a kid, my family used to say that my

younger sister Stacey was going to try to save the world, and "J.B. is going to try to buy it." They weren't far off. Here I was, almost forty years old, and nearly every person in my circle was through business. Why not? That was my source of pride and joy. I went out only if it was a networking opportunity; otherwise it was a waste of time. I didn't yearn to share my day's experience with someone who understood me for *me*. The only other piece that completed me was money.

I devoted 100 percent of my time to being an agent, which, because I require so little sleep, meant about twenty-two hours a day. My need for only one or two hours a night was the single biggest advantage in anything I had ever done, from high school to my first job as an assistant account executive on Procter & Gamble accounts at Grey Advertising. It was a purely natural gift; even as a little baby, I didn't require sleep. My dad, Larry, a toy industry executive, would drive me around our neighborhood of Huntington, Long Island, at all hours of the night in a futile attempt to knock me out. He and my mother, Carol, gave up trying to get me to go to bed after my maternal grandmother bought me a little black-and-white TV set with three channels and a headphone plug that had only one earpiece.

Grandma Ivy was a kindred spirit who stayed up late under the guise of cleaning and cooking (her two methods of currency were guilt and food), while my grandfather Abe was asleep every night at eight o'clock. When I stayed at her house in Flushing, Queens, which was often, I would come out at three in the morning to find her scrubbing the floors and eating a whole Entenmann's coffee cake. "It's not cut, even," she said before taking another chunk off the cake.

As a kid, I watched the TV set my grandma had gotten me—using the earpiece, so as not to disturb anyone—until Johnny Carson was over and the station literally went off the air. (I became deaf in my right ear from all the years of listening with the earpiece; if someone is talking on my right side, I can't hear what the hell they are saying.) Then I read the encyclopedia.

It wasn't insomnia; I just wasn't tired. Even as an adult, I always needed something else to fill my time while wide awake in the middle of the night. Instead of indulging in diversions to kill time, like eating Domino's pizza and playing *Call of Duty*, I decided to fill my head with the components of business ideas that could help my career. I read business journals from all around the world and analyzed trends in my field. I taped every show on prime-time TV—even ones that I had absolutely no interest in watching, like *Desperate Housewives*—so that I could see the commercials and extrapolate everything I needed to know about which brands were advertising and who they were marketing to. (I still do.) That way, if one of my athletes was asked to make a cameo on it, I could decide if it made sense.

With my single-minded devotion to work, no detail was too small if it might affect one of my clients. I saw my job as setting up the right deal and making sure that everything went the way it was set up. If Barry Sanders was starring in a Pepsi commercial, I not only negotiated the deal but also read the script, made his flight and hotel reservations, double-checked that his car arrived at the airport, and stocked the minifridge in his hotel room with his favorite drinks and fresh fruit. When Emmitt Smith was in a long-distance phone service commercial alongside ALF, the alien puppet star of the popular 1980s TV sitcom about a crash-landed extraterrestrial living with a suburban family, I went out in advance to talk to the puppeteer who operated the character. It had been a tough deal selling Emmitt on a national ad campaign that required him to appear with a puppet. The last thing I needed was for ALF to make him uncomfortable. "It's weird enough that Emmitt is this football god talking to a doll," I said to the puppeteer. "I don't want any bizarre stuff."

Because my love life didn't get any more serious than the brunette I picked up at the stadium, I didn't have any personal distractions to take my focus away from my clients. I didn't have to go home for Valentine's Day or duck out for a Little League game. In fact, I thought nothing of picking up my life and moving to wherever it best suited my business. In 2002, when Emmitt was approaching the all-time career rushing record set by Walter Payton, I moved from Miami to Dallas for two and a half years. I set up my office adjacent to the Cowboys' training facility so that I could deal with the fifty or so product deals we had going at one time. I spent Thanksgiving at his house and carried his sleeping kids up to their hotel room during the Super Bowl. I relocated to San Francisco in 2004. Three years later, when Barry Bonds started breaking all his MLB records, including the most career home runs, I made myself available to him 24/7, from driving to and from Giants games, to personally delivering rough cuts of ESPN's *Bonds on Bonds* reality TV show for his review at six o'clock every Tuesday morning. At Lions games, I was down on the sideline during halftime festivities making sure that Barry Sanders's three boys didn't get trampled by players exiting the field.

I fell somewhere between a concierge (recommending good golf courses to play during family vacations) and a member of the family (buying a table at the charity dinner run by one of my clients' mothers). I loved my job more than anything else in my life, but I never mistook it for fun. Just because I was in the room when something cool was happening didn't mean that it was a party for me.

Nothing could have been cooler than when I accompanied Barry Bonds to Jay-Z's 40/40 Club in New York City. Barry will tell you that *we* had the best night hanging out with Jay-Z and Beyoncé. The hip-hop mogul and Barry did have an awesome time, talking and laughing for hours in a *V*-VIP room—while I stood next to the door all night to make sure that no one bothered them.

I rode the coattails of greatness, working behind the scenes to make money off moments that others simply enjoyed. In 1994, when ice hockey great Wayne Gretzky broke the all-time goal record with his 802nd score, the scene was pure exuberance. Champagne was drunk straight from bottles and poured over Wayne's head as he ripped off and tossed his hockey shirt and his teammates hoisted him onto their shoulders. Then there was me, scurrying underfoot with a few security guys I'd hired to gather the used game clothes, shoes, and equipment and to iron on tamper-proof holograms to authenticate them for Upper Deck. Awesome.

I felt lucky to be in the room, but I was just completely stressed out. It was the same reason I couldn't watch sports with the same emotional investment I'd had as a kid. Whether it was baseball or badminton, I was always thinking about business.

Almost every year, I went to the Super Bowl with one of my clients—and almost every year, I flew home before the game started. Most people would have killed (or paid untold amounts of money) to watch the game from one of the luxury boxes or the kind of seats that I had access to. But after having arrived the Tuesday before the game and accompanying my client to (and smoothing out) appearances night and day right up to game day, I was wiped out by Sunday. Grateful for the empty airport that would be transformed into a zoo the next day with untold thousands of people traveling, I headed home uneventfully.

Super Bowl Sunday usually falls on or around my birthday, February 5, and my favorite way to celebrate was alone at home on my couch with the game and a pizza—or some other form of takeout. I literally could not have told you if my stove even worked.

*   *   *

In general, being a salesman—the essence of an agent—is the toughest thing one can do, because virtually every answer is "no." It takes a lot of creativity, stamina, and confidence. When I heard that two-letter word, I understood it as "not yet." I just hadn't answered all the person's questions yet, but I would. *No* meant *maybe*. And being a salesman who traded in seven figures, I was selling myself as much as any product or service. With that kind of money at stake, I had to prove beyond the shadow of a doubt that

I knew everything in this one arena and could help an athlete or corporation look good while making a mint.

Selling myself to new clients took up almost as much of my time as selling the ones already on my roster. When I flew out to the hometown of a big-time college running back who had finally decided to declare for the NFL draft, it was the culmination of two long years of a one-sided courtship. I couldn't talk to him about business during that whole time, because it would violate National Collegiate Athletic Association (NCAA) rules, but I had many long conversations and email exchanges with his parents about the kind of agent I was and would be for their son. Because of my pedigree, client roster, and the vision I outlined for them, they felt I was the natural choice to represent him.

As I touched down and then picked up my rental car, I was getting more and more amped. Finalizing a deal, particularly one that was two years in the making, is always a thrill. But this one was especially exciting because although my other clients were already A-listers by the time they'd signed with me, here was a chance to build an image from the ground up. I was champing at the bit to finally sit down with him and his dad to go over the real details that we hadn't previously been able to discuss (about how we would build his brand). How many nights had I spent coming up with plans for everything from this kid's logo to a tiered system of corporate sponsors? I had everything neatly organized in a binder: spreadsheets, designs, facts and figures. While I had no problem taking corporate clients on VIP visits to the Playboy Mansion, at heart I was still a massive nerd: the kid who stayed up all night reading the encyclopedia.

I had the athlete and his dad eating up my pitch for more than an hour when I decided to pull the trigger and suggest that we go ahead and sign the papers.

"Definitely. You are the perfect guy for me," the kid said, smiling from ear to ear. "All I need is a million-dollar signing bonus."

Wait, what? Maybe I had misheard. Maybe he had mixed up the term "signing bonus" for something else. It is not unheard of for an athlete in a tough financial situation to ask for an advance on money he'll make in endorsements and contracts, which he agrees to pay back with interest. But this kid, who came from a solid middle-class family and had a full ride to college, didn't appear to be in financial distress.

"What do you mean?" I asked. "You need a million advance against your contract or something?"

"No, a million bucks cash. In a duffel bag. No one needs to know about it. But that's what it's gonna take to get this done."

I'm usually a fast talker and can spin any situation. But

this demand left me speechless. A million bucks in a duffel bag? I wasn't hiring a hit man. Even if I wanted to give him a million dollars, how could I do that without letting the IRS know?

"Who gave you the idea that would be possible?"

He said something about another agent. That's when I stood up, closed the binder, put it and the contract I had prepared back in my briefcase, shook everyone's hand, and explained this wasn't the right fit for me.

"If there is anything else I can ever do for you, let me know," I said and left.

The kid's father chased me out to my rental car. "What's the matter?" he asked, genuinely confused by my quick exit. I didn't know what to say.

"Sir, I don't do business in that manner."

In my car to the airport, on the plane, back to my apartment, and all night long, I stewed: two and a half years of recruiting in the toilet. I had wasted all that time, energy, and money—as did the athlete. If he would have just signed with me, within a month I could have gotten him way more than $1 million in endorsements. I had thought this was a good kid, and he *was* a good kid. But the culture around sports in this country bred greed and an above-the-law attitude. I'm sure another agent *did* promise him $1 million cash, tax free.

I offered athletes a lot of value. I took pride in my

results and track record. There had to be people out there who could understand the skill set and work ethic I possessed and wouldn't ask me for $1 million in a freakin' duffel bag. There had to be a way I could find guys with earning potential *and* appreciation—even if it meant more work on my part. I didn't mind hard work. I lived for it. But I needed more control of my product. There had to be a better way.

My indignation and dissatisfaction didn't dissipate, despite my effort to distract myself out at clubs with hot girls. Night after night, I burned with anger. It fueled my brain that turned over ideas as quickly as the images flashed across the TV I kept on in the background all hours of the day and night.

During the National Basketball Association's 2006 All-Star Game, I was struck by Yao Ming's steely presence. The Houston Rockets' seven-foot-six center had grown into one of the top centers in the league, but in the last couple of years, he had missed a lot of games due to foot problems. Still, he was an international fan favorite and had the most fan votes going into the All-Star Game. I knew his agent, who had become wildly rich from the Chinese player's success. Yao Ming, who made *Forbes* lists, was bringing in $50 million a year easy.

As I watched Yao play, the formula for his success appeared before my eyes as clearly as if it were written on a chalkboard. He was the first person from a country with more than a billion people to be successful on an American professional team sport. Plus, the country he came from already had the pipeline in place (broadcasters, live-event ticket sales, sponsors, licensed merchandise production, and sales outlets) to monetize a pro athlete's worth.

While the night wore on, I became more fixated on the idea of replicating this formula. Where was my Yao Ming? ESPN hummed in the background while I went over a few contracts—busywork—when something else caught my attention.

The sports network was airing a cricket match in India; filler for the three-in-the-morning time slot. According to the radar gun on the screen, guys were throwing 150 kilometers per hour, or about 93 mph. A lightbulb went off.

From my foreign business journal reading, I knew there were something like 150 million Indian men between the ages of fifteen and twenty-five. And there were no college or pro teams in any sport scouting for talent there like they do in the United States. There was a pro cricket league, the Ranji Trophy, but the money was poor; only a national team really gave its players the opportunity for a career. As a result, there were a grand total of twenty-five pro sports jobs of note in a country with over a billion people.

What if I could tap into the undiscovered talent in India, import it to this country, and translate it into a great baseball pitcher?

Cricket and baseball pitching were not exactly apples and apples. On one hand, the cricket pitchers had the advantage of a running start. However, they were pitching on a flat surface and throwing on a bounce, unlike baseball pitchers who throw from a mound and directly to the catcher squatting behind home plate, sixty feet and six inches away.

I had heard many pitching coaches say, "Give me *anyone* who throws a hundred miles an hour, and I will give you a pitcher." Somebody over there had to have a strong arm. More than just somebody. Based on statistics alone, there had to be ten or fifteen thousand guys in India with the raw talent to pitch in the major leagues.

I went back to my Yao Ming formula and tested my new theory. India had the infrastructure to monetize a sports athlete through cricket, which was followed by millions of devoted fans. Also, no native athlete had ever become successful in any American pro sport. Suddenly, something out of left field was hurtling toward a logical and potentially very profitable conclusion.

How to find this hidden talent quickly presented itself as a problem: because no one in India had heard of baseball let alone played it, US scouts didn't go there. Why would they? There were no leagues. There weren't even games.

My mind skipped to yet another universe far from both India and Major League Baseball: *American Idol*. In the ultimate democratization of talent, judges go from city to city searching for diamond singers in the rough, with the tryouts promoted on all the local radio stations. The promise of being on television and possibly achieving stardom and winning a big prize gives the talent competition all the credibility and incentive it needs.

That was it! I would create an *American Idol*–style TV show aimed at finding young Indian men who had the physical tools to become MLB pitchers. Instead of a microphone, there would be a radar gun, and instead of a record deal, a major-league contract.

I wasted no time in setting up a pitch meeting to a pair of venture capitalists with an avid interest in sports. As soon as the hour turned civilized, I called Will Chang's office. Having met the famed Chinese American businessman through Barry Bonds following his investment firm's purchase of an equity stake in the San Francisco Giants, I wanted to bring him this idea that was so far out of left field it had left the park entirely. It wasn't because he was a Harvard grad or one of the most successful Asian investors in American sports. It wasn't even because he was a big promoter of US-Asian relations through a number of business organizations that he either founded or headed up. It was because he is a risk taker.

Will's corner office in the San Mateo, California, office building he owned was filled with sports memorabilia. An imposing guy hovering around six foot three, he shook my hand vigorously before padding back in his terry-cloth slippers to the big leather chair behind his gigantic chairman-style desk. I sat down on the other side of the desk next to Ash Vasudevan, the Indian-born managing partner of a venture capital fund focusing on new ventures in tech, sports, and entertainment. He was Will's right-hand man in a lot of businesses.

As I unfolded my outlandish plan, the koi fish in Will's large tank darted in and out of the driftwood. I hadn't even started in on the *American Idol*–style TV show part when Will jumped in with high energy typical of the rich and powerful.

"See, Ash, this is *exactly* what I am talking about," he said. "We can find a freak of nature. We have all the Yao Ming capabilities in this thing."

The look on my face must have shown my confusion, because Will went on to explain his philosophy about the super-abilities of top athletes. It seemed that Will had run in a marathon once, and despite training hard, he couldn't do better than six hours. Meanwhile, the best runner completed the race in two. His frustration as an athlete led him to believe that certain people are endowed with special gifts of physicality.

"It's a lot harder to find a Yao Ming, someone from out in the sticks who can walk onto the court and play like a professional, than it is to find someone who has just the raw talent," observed Ash. He had played cricket in India from the time he could walk all the way up through the equivalent of the sport's minor leagues.

"If you can't find a Yao Ming, can you create one?" Will asked me.

I used probability as my proof. Out of twenty million to thirty million men of recruitable age in the United States, we have thousands of pro athletes, as well as about ten thousand with the ability but who crapped out because of injuries or circumstances.

"Do the math," I said. "How many do you think there are among one hundred fifty million where no one is being recruited? Baseball has no value over there. Even if someone could throw fast, no one would know."

"That's it!" Will cried. "India isn't undertalented but underrecruited. Their superhuman athletes are right now working the fields or for UPS. This will be easy if we have the right execution."

We decided to hold the contest in India. That was going to be our play. When I left Will's office that day, the level of optimism was off the charts. The three of us felt like we couldn't fail.

Unfortunately, it seemed that Will and Ash were the only ones who thought the idea was a good one. I was ridiculed by other people in the business as soon I started to discuss a reality-show-style baseball talent search in India.

I heard the same thing from everybody I talked to: no way was this going to work! No matter what I may have accomplished in the past, this idea was going to kill my career.

A good friend of mine who worked for a sports video-game company took me aside. "J.B.," he said, "I know you have made a lot of crazy ideas work in the past, but this is the absolute worst idea I have ever heard in my life."

A baseball team owner cautioned that the idea was so bad that if I were smart, I would find a way to back out before I ruined my relationship with Will. A top exec at MLB International, the arm of the MLB Association that runs baseball everywhere outside the United States, said I was just wasting my time and money; that India would never yield talent.

As I set about making my mission a reality, I heard every stereotype in the book. Most of the people I talked to had never set foot in India, and yet they were convinced that all the guys there were five foot two and unathletic. They conjured up images of small guys doing tech support in outsourcing centers. "What about the Great Khali, the Indian wrestler in the WWE?" I argued. "He's seven foot one and three hundred fifty pounds." They just looked at me like I was crazy.

No matter what anybody said, I never wavered. Even if the percentage of people above six feet was much lower in India than in the United States, simple math dictated that India would still have more people above six feet because it had a much larger general population. Math would never let me down.

Now, as Will said, I just needed the right execution.

CHAPTER 2

Six months after my initial meeting with Will and Ash, I was on a flight bound for India to try launching the contest.

Stepping off my plane in Mumbai at two o'clock in the morning on November 15, 2007, I was instantly overcome by the heat. The air was thick, moist, and pungent. After the antiseptic cool of the two-leg, twenty-two-hour flight, I could hardly breathe it was so stifling. The airport obviously wasn't air-conditioned.

As I made my way to the baggage claim, sweat circles spread out under my arms, on my back, and across my chest. Everywhere I looked, there were banks of pay phones. Most of them were filled with women in colorful saris and men in short-sleeved dress shirts, slacks, and sandals making calls. It was like I had stepped off a time machine to thirty years ago.

When I got downstairs to pick up my luggage, the noise hit me before anything else. With about ten international flights all about to land at the same time, large families carrying enough luggage to last a lifetime or two, official-looking men blowing whistles, little children playing tag, and old women crying, it was like walking into some crazy after-hours bazaar. In my experience, airports are typically empty in the early hours of the morning. But this one was filled with more activity than I had ever seen anywhere else, ever. I muscled my way to the baggage carousel, grabbed my bags as soon as they came around, and found the automatic doors, desperate to escape the chaos.

But when I got outside, I found only more chaos—and more heat. There were people everywhere, holding signs and screaming. "Do you need a car, sir?" "This way, sir!" "Sir!" "Sir?" "Sir!"

I searched frantically for my driver. I had assumed there would be a guy standing with a sign bearing my name, the same as when you fly into anywhere else, and my assumption wasn't wholly incorrect. Except in this case, there were literally *hundreds* of guys holding signs. To make it even more confusing, 90 percent of them clearly worked for the same company, because they were all wearing the exact same white driver's coat, pants, and hat. It was like walking into an endless sea of ice-cream vendors.

The heat, the noise, the ice-cream-vendor army: it was total sensory overload, and I had been on Indian soil for only a few minutes.

After stumbling around and rapidly dehydrating, I finally located my driver and collapsed in the backseat of his Toyota Innova minivan, but my relief was short lived.

The forty-five-minute drive to my hotel was lined almost entirely with shantytowns. The extreme poverty was marked even as we sped by—at one point, veering onto the wrong side of the road, in the direct path of cars heading right for us in what I was sure was going to be the end of my life. All just so that my driver could pass the car in front of us.

After sitting in an intersection for a nasty twenty-minute symphony of car horns beeping without pause, we arrived at the Taj President, a large high-rise overlooking the Indian Ocean. The upscale hotel was located in Cuffe Parade, the business district of Mumbai and one of the most exclusive neighborhoods with the plushest residences in all of India. Even then, upon exiting the car, I was besieged by a group of kids with no shirts or shoes (and some without teeth) hawking the most bizarre wares. The one closest to me was selling a copy of the magazine *Harvard Business Review,* a bouquet of plastic flowers, and a bunch of Rosetta Stone French language CDs. I felt like I was hallucinating.

Entering the lobby, I was revived by the familiarity of a luxury hotel (God bless air-conditioning). I approached the front desk, my typical confident stride returning.

"Hama kare, mein darj karna chahta hoon," I said in Hindi, which translated to "Excuse me, I would like to check in," followed by a flash of my winning smile.

Before leaving for India, I had tried to learn as much Hindi as I could, listening to language CDs while running or driving in the car. I was under no illusion that I was going to become fluent in Hindi; my studies were a matter of respect rather than utility. By this point in my life, I was fairly well traveled. While attending college at University of Massachusetts Amherst back in the 1980s, I used a Eurail pass to travel all over Europe, going as far east as Russia. And when I worked for Upper Deck, I went to South America to chase down the rights for a set of World Cup soccer trading cards. I had been to Japan on baseball business, and to Guangzhou, China, with Barry Sanders for NFL China, the arm of the NFL that handles sponsors, broadcasting, and merchandise in China.

In all my previous travels, I found it wasn't so important that I learn a language but that I *try* to learn it. My attempt to speak Hindi was proof that I wasn't an ethnocentric American.

But the young Indian man screwed up his face, clearly not having understood a word I said. I knew that Hindi was very different from English, but I didn't think my pronunciation had been that far from the throaty woman on the CD. I tried again. Now the concierge looked pained.

"Very sorry, sir," the clerk said in the most polite and perfect enunciation. "Do you perchance speak English?"

"Yes."

"Oh, thank God."

As I discovered, there are only a few cities in India where the modern standard Hindi I had been studying was in common use. Down south in Chennai, they speak Tamil. In Calcutta, it's Bengali. In Chandigarh, Punjabi. If I had wanted to chat with this guy in Mumbai, I should have learned Marathi. Or just speak English, as we did. Six months of Rosetta Stone was 100 percent worthless.

I hoped that the rest of my plan would prove a little more successful than my language studies. *Million Dollar Arm*—as Will, Ash, and I had coined our project—was to begin as a series of promotional events throughout the country that would drum up excitement for (or even just awareness of) the contest. Hopefully, having discovered some raw talent, we planned to hold qualifying trials in six different cities before the final competition and crowning of a champion.

Officially, we were looking for prospects between the ages of sixteen and twenty-five. But even in the best-case scenario, the athlete would have to train in the States in order to get signed and then put in a couple of years in the minors. So realistically, I didn't want to bring anyone older than twenty back to America to train for a tryout in front of all of Major League Baseball. From the start, we decided to bring the winner to the United States, along with anyone else who had a legitimate shot at playing pro baseball. Only the winner, however, would receive a cash prize of $100,000 during the finals—plus a chance to win $1 million if he could throw three consecutive strikes over 90 miles an hour.

First things first: I had to obtain permits to hold the promotional and qualifying events in India's public parks. To navigate the foreign business landscape, we had hired an advertising and promotions agency with a local office to help with the contest. My contacts at the agency were Sanjay Lal, the owner, who spent most of his time at his headquarters in Dubai; Vivek Daglur, who ran the office in Bangalore; and Vaibhav Bassi, my day-to-day assistant throughout the contest.

Vaibhav looked more like a scenester from Dubai than someone who hailed from northern India. In his crisp dress shirts, expensive driving mocs, and designer tortoiseshell glasses, he had an aura of upbeat cool. Vaibhav's reputation was that he was especially adept at talking to government officials and working the system—and I believed it. With his smooth way of talking and hip clothes, you couldn't help but want to ally yourself with him.

On the way to the municipal office to request a permit, Vaibhav talked about his interests, which matched his persona. Hot restaurants, hot clubs, hot stars—he was definitely in the mix. If this thing took off and I got invited to Bollywood events, he told me, I had to take him along.

The two of us walked into a large room painted gray, the international color of bureaucracy, where men in identical cubicles looked tired and hot. There were no signs, titles, or even names to guide us to the appropriate person to talk to about the park. Vaibhav, unperturbed by the lack of information, simply started talking to the man in the cubicle closest to the door as if the two were long-lost friends.

While Vaibhav described *Million Dollar Arm* and the permit we needed for guys to throw baseballs in the park, the clerk nodded enthusiastically, insisting that our needs were "no problem." My shoulders dropped from up around my ears where they had hovered since I arrived in this hectic country. The clerk really seemed to be on board when he told Vaibhav and me to have a seat. I relaxed in the hard plastic chair.

Ten minutes later, a man from an adjacent cubicle came out shaking his head and repeating, "This is impossible." My shoulders immediately rose back to their previously tense position, but Vaibhav acted like he knew the man was going to say that from the beginning. "There's nothing to get excited about, my friend," he said to the second man. "It's no big deal. We are talking about a few boys throwing around a few balls."

Who was this guy? Who was the first man that Vaibhav had talked to? Who was anybody? It never became clear to me, because it *wasn't* clear. In India, no one wants to let on who is in charge. Instead, they try to make it appear like everyone is equal. So in making your way through the massive amount of red tape, you have to go from person to person, getting the lowest person and each person above him to sign off on a plan or document until finally the highest official on the ladder is willing to sign. For someone like me, who hadn't asked anyone permission for anything since grade school, the process was maddening.

After a twenty-minute conversation with the second clerk, he gave us the next clue: the man that we needed to see was out for coffee and would be back in about ten minutes. Vaibhav and I returned to our seats and waited. I could feel my patience quickly wearing thin. When the same clerk reappeared about an hour later, I thought my head was going to explode.

"He is actually in a meeting out of the office," he said.

"But I thought you said he went to get a coffee?" I butted in angrily.

"*That* is where he is having coffee."

Vaibhav shot me a look to shut up. He was concerned that I would screw things up, and rightfully so. These were sensitive, strange, and precarious dealings. All it would take was for one guy to get a bad taste in his mouth to scuttle the deal.

After we left the municipal office, Vaibhav told me, "Next time, just stand there and look rich."

Four days and about fifty signatures later, we got the permit. That, however, was just the start to the complete insanity of doing business in India. While prepping for my trip, Will, Ash, and I had countless meetings about the type of talent we would be looking for, about branding, about the format of the TV show, and so many other details. But it never occurred to me that there wouldn't be high-speed internet available except in one small corner near the spa in my luxury hotel, or that my cell phone wouldn't work much of the time, and when it did, it would cost about $8 a second.

I also never considered the geopolitical implications of the pitching setup we had sent from the States. While the plan was always to have a lot of stuff for the contest and show—like T-shirts bearing the show's logo and baseballs—manufactured in India to save money, we had to bring the pitching cage, plate, mound, and a mannequin to stand in for a batter, all of which were made in America. Before packing up the mannequin, though, we dressed it in a baseball jersey and pants so that it wouldn't be naked, and those, I learned later, were made in China.

I was made aware of the origins of the clothing after an Indian customs agent discovered the "Made in China" labels, which turned into a huge headache for us. India's fraught relations with China made bringing anything from that country into India difficult. The mannequin's stupid outfit was holding up our shipment! Vaibhav had his work cut out for him getting our stuff into the country.

Making the baseballs in India proved to be an even bigger headache than our cheap Chinese-made baseball clothes. The process had started like all my other endeavors there: friendly and confident. When I showed a manufacturer an MLB regulation ball that I had brought with me, he told me in no uncertain terms, "I can make this, no problem." Fast-forward to a week before Vaibhav and I were scheduled to hit the road to promote *Million Dollar Arm.* The shipment arrived, but when I opened the box, I found three hundred cricket balls. Not cricket balls that looked like baseballs. Or baseballs that looked like cricket balls. Straight-up cricket balls. Cricket balls have a hard casing, and one seam that goes around the circumference of the ball, unlike the softer leather and dual-seam pattern on a baseball. They also weigh about half an ounce more.

"What the hell are these?" I bellowed. "I gave you the sample!"

"Oh yes, sir. We did not know what were those balls. So we made you cricket balls."

What was wrong with these people? It wasn't that in the United States we were any more competent. Sure, a lot of sports manufacturers in America would botch making cricket balls. But at least back home, we knew that when we messed up, we either had to admit it or try to cover it up. We didn't just change the plan when things didn't go right and expect the other party to accept it.

Everybody in India is so eager for work that he'll say anything to get business. Then he has no qualms about coming back and saying that he can't do what he said he was going to do. "It'll be done" is the common refrain, and utterly meaningless.

With the balls for *Million Dollar Arm*, it wasn't just a matter of nominal authenticity that made using cricket balls instead of baseballs a problem. This was a contest to bring back Indians who had a shot at the major leagues, and the only way to judge that was on speed. To do that, the balls had to be as close to an official MLB ball as possible. An ounce heavier could slow down a pitcher's speed by as much as seven miles an hour, with the opposite true as well. The average baseball weighs five ounces, while cricket balls could weigh at least a half ounce more. Meanwhile, my cricket-ball maker thought that his three hundred balls constituted a job well done.

We went through the same drill with the next manufacturer: "I can make this, no problem!" And then when we got the sample back, the balls were way too small.

When the balls from a third manufacturer arrived, they looked and felt perfect. The seams were in the right place, and the weight was five ounces on the nose. Then we took them out for a test drive. Vaibhav, who was as much a contender for the majors as my kid sister, threw one of the balls, which hit the ground and exploded. The seams were so fragile that they burst if the ball hit anything harder than the net, disintegrating into sawdust on impact.

We went through two more manufacturers before we finally got our baseballs. All this time, I was navigating this frustratingly inefficient terrain with the worst caffeine headache of my life. While I didn't drink coffee, I was a heavy user of Diet Coke. Back home, I was good for ten cans a day. But it wasn't so easy to find the stuff in India. Compared to exploding baseballs, nonexistent pitching equipment, and permit problems, this was a minor inconvenience. But when my temples were pounding, it felt like a big deal—and didn't exactly do great things for my increasingly bad mood.

I was particularly short tempered the morning of my meeting with a television executive to pitch our show. I still hadn't worked out a deal to make and air a reality show about *Million Dollar Arm*—the linchpin of the contest. Everything else had been such a pain in the ass, I couldn't imagine that this was going to be a piece of cake. I stopped at the concierge desk of my hotel and asked for a driver who could speak English and knew his way around the part of town where I was headed.

"No problem, sir, it will be done."

I got in the car and gave the address to the driver.

"Yes, yes," he replied.

"You know where that is?" I asked.

"Yes, yes."

The windows were rolled down, but the morning was anything but fresh.

"Do you have air-conditioning?"

"Yes, yes."

"Well, can you turn it on?"

"Yes, yes."

For Christ's sake, this guy didn't understand a word I was saying. He probably didn't have AC, either, so I sat back totally on edge while we bumped along the city's terrible streets, which were laid out so haphazardly I wondered how anyone got anywhere.

I shouldn't have wondered, because as it turned out, we *weren't* getting anywhere. After we had been in the car for an hour, suddenly my driver, without explanation (although, to be fair, he couldn't have explained to me anyway), pulled over and got out of the car. He approached a couple of men squatting over a rusty bicycle. They seemed to be talking forever when I got out and went up to them.

"No problem, sir. We help with directions," one of the squatting men said in English.

I asked if he knew the location of the TV network's

office. No, he informed me proudly, but they had given the driver directions to a man named Amid three blocks away. *He* would know. I thought I was going to cry.

"You said you knew where you were going!" I yelled, pointing my finger at my driver. We all looked at the English speaker to translate.

"Well," the driver replied once he understood, "I'm in the right city, aren't I?"

I wanted to catch a cab back to the States. But there was nothing to do but get back in the car and find Amid, which we did, and a half hour later, we pulled up to an enormous fifty-story building of glass and steel with an incongruous dirt driveway that looked like it should be in a rural village somewhere and not leading up to a skyscraper. Jaguars and Range Rovers were covered in its red dust.

"Okay, I have a meeting," I said to the driver, using my hands to mime my words. "Wait [*holding out my palm, indicating "Stop"*] here [*pointing downward*]. I'll be out [*walking fingers*] in one hour [*index finger*]."

True to my word, I was back outside in an hour on the dot. (Anyone who knows me knows that I am never late.) The dirt road had become a busy street with dust hanging in the air like a hot red cloud. I looked left and right but didn't immediately see the car. I could see child beggars starting to approach. All I wanted to do was get in the car.

Where the hell was my driver? A little kid in nothing but a loincloth held up for sale a Motorola cell phone charger and a squirt gun.

My eyes watered in the heat and dust while I called the driver's cell number that I had taken for just this very reason. It rang and rang until a recorded message in Hindi said, "The cell phone you are trying to reach is switched off." (In 2007 virtually no one used voice mail in India; if someone didn't pick up, you were out of luck. Even now, they text instead.)

What was I supposed to do? I felt helpless in a way that would have been inconceivable for me back in America. But in America, this whole situation would be inconceivable. After a Mercedes, picking up some Saudi execs, took off and coated me with a layer of dirt, I turned to the driver of another car to ask where drivers parked around here. I found the congregated cars six blocks away and, about fifteen minutes later, my driver. It turned out that he had gone to get some tea. "You said you were going to be an hour?" he said unapologetically, although it had been an hour and forty-five minutes when I finally tracked him down.

An hour is more ambiguous in India than it is in America. *Everything* is more ambiguous in India.

I am not a guy who gets homesick, but back in my hotel room, looking out at the cold, black Indian Ocean, this place felt too big, too crazy, too much. I knew myself to be someone who could work a room, understand the subtlest dynamic, and turn it to my advantage. Here, I didn't even understand how to take a cab.

It wasn't just that I was out of my element; it was also how in-your-face everything was here. What is usually kept hidden in other countries flourishes out in the open without apology in India—like the shantytowns nestled among skyscrapers that reach seventy stories and beyond. Many countries maintain stark boundaries between their rich and poor, but in India the juxtaposition of the two was unsettling. The shantytowns around the skyscrapers were inhabited by the buildings' construction workers from faraway villages, who preferred to live under tarps and pieces of metal siding than to eat up their meager wages commuting to and from work.

Even in the quiet cocoon of my high-rise hotel room, I couldn't escape the reality of the human condition. From my window, I could see the slums that lined the ocean side of the highway below. Remember that the Taj President Hotel was located in Cuffe Parade, one of the most expensive areas in all of India, where high-rises on the land side of the coast-hugging highway boasted apartments that went for $40 million to $50 million. Yet their immediate neighbors on the other side of the highway lived in shacks of Sheetrock and aluminum held together with duct tape on a shore covered in plastic bags, shreds of clothing, pieces of paper, cans, and all manner of trash. Goats picked their way atop boat hulls steps away from a man parking his Maybach.

Yes, I believed in math—but math couldn't make sense of what I had experienced since arriving in India.

Still, what choice did I have other than to continue on with this crazy idea? I couldn't hop a flight home and tell Will and Ash that things got too weird and difficult over here. Plus, I'm sure that Vaibhav would have talked me out of it even if I wanted to—that guy could talk anybody out of or into anything. No, I had to see this through to the end.

I had to get used to India, and that included how it did business on a handshake alone. Even the deal with the sports network to produce and air *Million Dollar Arm* was made on a simple verbal agreement, not unlike the one I had with the first baseball maker.

When I explained to Himanshu Modi, the head of Zee Sports, what I had in mind for the show, his response was, "It will be done."

"We are envisioning eight episodes," I continued.

"It will be done."

That sentence was really beginning to bug me. TV was going to get out the word about *Million Dollar Arm* better than I or the agency ever could. And, more importantly, it was going to tell kids that this contest was legit. Otherwise I would just be some American standing in the local park with a sign and a radar gun.

"We want to start running the episodes two or three weeks behind each of the main qualifier events, to give you time to edit. Then you'll air the finals."

"Very good."

In a matter of minutes, we had it all worked out. I shook Modi's hand and told him to send me a contract.

"No," he said. "No contracts necessary."

"No offense, but I prefer to have something in writing."

But he did take offense. In fact, he thought I was saying that I didn't trust him, which technically *was* true. I don't trust anybody. As far as I was concerned, that's what contracts are for.

After a conversation with Ash, who explained how business works in India and said not to sweat the contract, Zee Sports became our TV network. Not in my wildest imagination could I have envisioned signing up a show to a TV station like that. No paperwork. Only a handshake and an "It will be done."

Well, I certainly hoped so.

CHAPTER 3

San Francisco Giants star closer Brian Wilson, wearing a full suit and dress shoes, released a clean fastball as loose and easy as if he were playing a game of catch. The radar gun clocked it at a cool 80 mph. Since it was the off-season, Wilson was reluctant to throw full throttle, so he made some light tosses to illustrate the mechanics of pitching instead.

Reporters and cameramen from twenty-five or so media outlets assembled outside a Mumbai horse racetrack for the press conference to kick off *Million Dollar Arm* looked on blankly as Wilson's pitches rocketed past them. They had no idea what they were watching. No point of comparison. The great turnout for a story about a sport that most of them had a very limited understanding of could be explained by the fact that after Brian's demonstration, we held a contest to see which reporter could throw the fastest: whoever had the best arm in the media would win up to 10,000 rupees, or roughly $160.

With each reporter's try at the cash prize, Brian's skill became more and more apparent to the crowd, which, like the rest of India, consisted almost exclusively of cricket fans. Some of them couldn't even get the ball in the cage. A pitching cage is similar to a batting cage, a netted-in area the distance between the pitching mound and home plate, with a painted catcher and batter at one end to help practice throwing. Missing the pitching cage entirely, the wild pitches sent the rest of us ducking for cover. And most of them were throwing almost impossibly slowly; I mean 20 mph slow. Based on my experience, not one man in the entire Indian media can throw anywhere close to a 70 mph fastball.

The reporters could have thrown 5-mile-per-hour fastballs, for all I cared. Whether it's in India, the United States, or Antarctica, when it comes to the media, I have three jobs. The first is to get them interested enough to show up for an event. The second is to make the experience of covering the event positive enough that it will be favorably treated in their story. And the third is to make sure their story is accurate. Well, with *Million Dollar Arm*, at least I got two out of three.

When I opened the newspapers the following day, I couldn't believe my eyes. More than a few of the Indian journalists had confused Brian Wilson, the famed relief pitcher, with Brian Wilson, leader of the Beach Boys. It seemed that someone's Google search had gone horribly awry. Even though the singer-songwriter was sixty-five years old, that didn't send up red flags for the writers who had seen Brian (described in one article as "America's number one death pitcher," whatever that meant) in the flesh throw a fastball.

The case of the mistaken Brian Wilson identity was just the first in a long comedy of errors, as Vaibhav and I went on the road for the next several months in search of at least one good arm.

From the start, the entire *Million Dollar Arm* project had been conceived of as a numbers game. The more young men who were aware that they could win $1 million, the more of them would try out. And the more people who tried out, the better chance we had of finding some legitimate prospects to bring home to train for a spot in the major leagues.

To that end, I spent from dawn to dusk in one park or another across India as we traveled nonstop, holding events in as many different places as possible. "Parks" was a loose term for where we passed our days. In India, most parks are just dirt fields without a blade of grass in sight. When kids get out of school, they head to the closest park to play cricket. And the kids who don't go to school, of which there are many, occupy the park every day from morning to night. They don't even need a park, or equipment, for that matter: Indian kids will fill in any empty spaces they find to play the country's national pastime. In Mumbai's Shivaji Park, it's common to find ten thousand people playing cricket—some using rocks and sticks, and others with professional gear. There are so many kids playing at once on the park's twenty-seven acres that the games physically overlap. A guy playing outfield in one game will be standing right next to a guy playing outfield in another. Typical Indian chaos.

In any given park, we set up our *Million Dollar Arm* outpost in one corner of the field, so that we were off to the side. We weren't going to make any friends disturbing people's cricket games. Once we had camped for the day, we hired kids to run through the park, handing out informational flyers and yelling, "Go on TV and win a million dollars!" As soon as a cricket match ended, our hired guns ran after the players to encourage them to stop at the pitching cage on their way out. No one was breaking up a cricket game to throw a baseball, that's for sure.

Until I actually saw it with my own eyes in parks across India, I didn't have a full understanding of how truly massive cricket is in that country. Technically, field hockey is the national sport of India, but cricket is the national obsession. The sports section of any newspaper is devoted almost entirely to cricket, with one page for all other sports, from soccer, to basketball, to chess. At any given time, it's likely that all seven of India's dedicated sports channels are showing cricket. On one channel, you can watch live cricket, and then if you get bored, you can flip to another and watch some classic match from 1990 in which India beat Australia. On the next channel, they'll have the World Eighteen-and-Under Cricket Championships, or something like that, and then, on the next one, some old prerecorded match between Sri Lanka and Australia. It doesn't even matter if it's an Indian team: the country's insatiable desire to watch cricket knows no geographical or demographical bounds.

The only way to compare it to America is to think about football, which is far and away our most popular sport. Still, there is a limit to how much football people in the United States are interested in watching. Imagine if, all year round, on all the different sports channels, they showed nothing but live NFL games, old NFL games, college games, high school games, Pop Warner games, and so on. That's what cricket is like in India. There *is* an ESPN channel in India that airs live Major League Baseball games at three o'clock in the morning, because of the time difference. But the network allots the game only a certain time slot, and when it's over, so is baseball. In the ninth inning of a nail-biter, it will cut out, and viewers are suddenly enjoying the cricket news report.

India's devotion to cricket borders on cultlike. Every day at five o'clock, thousands gather outside the home of Kapil Dev, a retired cricket superstar who in 2007 held just about every record in the sport and who endorses all kinds of products (including particular brands of cement and rebar), for a quick glimpse of and wave from the cricket god.

When it comes to professional athletics, the cricket blinders mean very little opportunity for most anyone who wants to make his or her living playing sports. In the United States, there are thousands and thousands of pros in dozens of different leagues and events, from the NFL, to the UFC (Ultimate Fighting Championship), to the X Games. In India, a nation with over 150 million boys, the sum total of sports careers where the player had any chance of making good money was twenty-five spots on the national cricket team. And some of the guys on the cricket team have been on it for twenty years!

The odds that a kid who could throw a baseball would win the $1 million was way, way higher than getting a spot on the national cricket team. The only problem was that it didn't seem like any of the kids in India could actually throw a baseball.

When the kids pitched, it was a train wreck: 99 percent terrible, 100 percent crazy. They were so bad that more often than not someone watching got hit with a ball. The first time that a skinny teenager in a dusty school uniform launched the ball a good ten feet to the left of the net, I almost didn't believe my eyes. *How the hell did he miss a twenty-foot net?* In America you would have never seen a ball thrown that wildly, even by little kids. But in India, it happened all the time: to the left or right, or high in the air like a golf ball whistling down the fairway.

Of course, it's pretty understandable. If someone is hurling a ball as hard as he can but doesn't know when to release it, because he's never done it before, where that ball is headed is anyone's guess. It became so commonplace that I decided my place in the contest was right behind the pitcher. No one was so bad that he could throw it *behind* him.

Vaibhav, who knew just as much about baseball as our contestants, wasn't quite as strategic about his safety. Before I came along, he was aware that baseball was a sport but had never seen it played. Still, every now and then I caught him showing kids how to throw a baseball. "No, no, no, don't do that," I scolded. "Stick to what you know."

All I needed was these kids getting baseball tips from Vaibhav.

He should have listened, because he wound up with a ball in his face. After one of the kids had his turn, a ball had gone rogue, rolling about forty feet left of the pitching cage, and another contestant in line chased it down. Vaibhav, instead of letting him run back with the ball, as he should have done, held out his hands and shouted unwisely, "Throw it here!"

As the words came out of his mouth, I wondered, *Why is he doing that?* But by the time the thought fully formed in my head, it was too late. Just as these kids didn't know when to release the ball, they also didn't know how to throw it gently. The contestant whipped it at Vaibhav, who caught it with his head. Out of all the countless people who got hit with balls during the contest, Vaibhav was the only one who took it in the face. (The others got hit in the back of the head because they weren't looking.) His fancy designer glasses shattered, and he ended up needing stitches.

Vaibhav proved just as adroit with the baseball equipment as he was with the game itself. While we were in the city of Indore, midway between Mumbai and New Delhi, our radar gun stopped working. After bringing it to a handyman, who charged me $500 and then told me he couldn't fix it—most likely because he'd never seen a radar gun in his life—we resorted to using balls with little LED screens that marked the speed. But they turned out to be completely inaccurate (off by plus or minus 10 mph, according to the manufacturer) and, so, completely worthless.

Vaibhav said that the real problem was with the generator used to provide power out in the parks and to our radar gun (because of the difference in voltage between the United States and India). Now, Vaibhav's real skill was talking. He was so authoritative, even the crankiest government officials came around to his side. So when he said the problem was with the generator, I went for it, hook, line, and sinker.

Ash shipped in a brand-new Yamaha generator. In the week and a half it took to arrive, I was going out of my mind over the time we were wasting. In this numbers game, ours were dwindling every minute. After the new generator arrived, it was held up again in customs because a government official worried about its environmental impact. Now, India is by no means a pristine eco habitat; there is pollution everywhere. Untold millions of three-wheelers belch filth into the sky out of go-kart engines built back in the 1970s. People use rivers as garbage dumps. But according to this official, our top-of-the-line generator was going too far.

It wasn't a surprise. Anytime you ask anyone in power in India for anything, the first answer is *"Namumakin,"* which in Hindi means "impossible." Enter Vaibhav, who went to see the official and talked him into handing over our generator.

Unfortunately, after the new generator was set up, the radar gun still didn't work. I went over to see for myself what was happening and was horrified by what I found. Under Vaibhav's careful guidance, his crack team had cut the American-style plugs off the radar gun and stuck the wires—with the plugs snipped off—into the outlets on the generator (made for American-style plugs). Twigs held the wires in the holes.

Surveying the Frankensteinian situation, a terrifying thought occurred to me: *What does Vaibhav know about mechanical equipment?* After I spliced the plug back on, wrapping it with electrical tape, and then plugged it into the new generator, the gun *still* didn't work. Now, I'm not exactly the handiest guy in the world, but I asked if anybody had checked the fuse. Everybody looked at me, like, *What's a fuse?*

Between the repairs and the customs fees and the new generator, not only did I lose over a week's worth of time, I also spent $14,000 to fix a problem that could have been solved with a 50-cent fuse.

Vaibhav was incredibly intelligent and even more loyal, but he always seemed to get tripped up by the simple things. This special quality of his almost landed my entire team, including me, in jail. It all began on an early Sunday morning as we were setting up for a tryout in Calcutta's Jodhpur Park, when the mounted military police questioned our operation but ultimately, after Vaibhav chatted with them, left us alone.

No sooner had we finished setting up the large net, pitcher's mound, mannequin, and display board when a whole other contingent of police in completely different

uniforms—this time from the Calcutta municipal force—
asked to see our permit. According to them, it was no
good, despite the fifty municipal officials who'd signed off
on it. But worse than that, the police lieutenant placed us
under arrest for unlawful assembly and called a police bus
(a school bus with bars on the windows) to confiscate all
our equipment. We had gone from reality show producers
to outlaws in five minutes flat.

Vaibhav sprung into action, needling and cajoling the
lieutenant into telling us what we had to do to avoid going
to jail. Surprisingly, to me at least, there was a way: we
needed permission from a certain ranking officer, known
ominously as Colonel Q, who happened to work on the
military base directly across the street from the park.

"Give us one hour," Vaibhav said dramatically.

The police lieutenant agreed, as long as we left our
staff and stuff with him as a guarantee of our return. Our
driver raced us across the road and across the street to
the base. Vaibhav sweet-talked our way onto the base—
even though what good could two strangers be up to at
seven o'clock on a Sunday morning?—and convinced an
assistant in the main office to call and bother this Colonel Q at just such an early hour on a weekend morning. As he explained the situation over the phone to the
colonel, I worried that we were going to be drawn and
quartered.

Instead, a half hour later, the door flew open, and in marched Colonel Q, a tiny man covered in medals that together probably weighed more than he did. And boy, was he angry—except not at us. "Give me this guy's number," he said to Vaibhav.

As he dialed the ranking police officer's number from his cell and gave it to Colonel Q for a serious tongue-lashing, I had to hand it to Vaibhav. He had really come through on this one. "You got me out of bed because somebody wants to throw a ball around in the park?" the Colonel screamed into the phone. "You let these guys do whatever they want, unless you want to spend the rest of the day emptying garbage cans!"

Back in the car, I gloated to our driver, "The situation is resolved. Colonel Q approved our permit."

"I know," the driver said. "I just spoke to him."

"What do you mean *you* just spoke to him?"

When Vaibhav went to call the police lieutenant, he'd misdialed and called our driver by mistake. Colonel Q's diatribe was so intimidating that the driver hadn't uttered a single word to let him know he was screaming at the wrong guy.

The scene at the park was mayhem. The police, who had *not* received the message that we were allowed to stay, had put my entire staff in handcuffs. And as soon as Vaibhav and I returned, we were put in handcuffs, too.

"You're making a big mistake!" Vaibhav yelled. "If I'm wrong, you can put me in jail forever!"

I was contemplating what a jail cell in Calcutta would be like while Vaibhav continued to plead with the lieutenant to let him make just one phone call to Colonel Q. If he was lying, the lieutenant would know right away, and we would go to jail anyway. But if he wasn't, the lieutenant would be in big trouble for carting us away.

He relented—probably just to get Vaibhav to shut up—and called the military base himself. As the colonel's assistant on the other end of the line relayed the entire conversation that had been delivered to my driver by accident and explained why he probably wouldn't want to bother the colonel for a second time on a Sunday morning, the police lieutenant's face turned white, and he began whispering to all the other cops, "Uncuff them! Uncuff them!"

It was all in a day's work. In leaving no stone unturned in my search for pitchers, I experienced more of India than most Indians will ever see in their lifetime. The conditions of our travels were as varied as the different landscapes: from the clean, industrialized city of Bangalore, where all the big international technology companies are headquartered; to the lush rain forests of Karnataka; to Ludhiana in the state of Punjab, where the pollution is so bad that you can cut the air with a knife.

Our hotel accommodations were equally diverse. In Hyderabad, we stayed at a Taj hotel that was once a nineteenth-century palace built in the shape of a scorpion. While in the small town of Madhubani, we had to keep going down to the front desk and buying scratch-off cards in order to use the internet.

No matter where we went, however, my first order of business was getting a supply of Diet Coke. Whenever I checked into one of the hotels from the Taj chain, I had the staff clear out the minibar and stock it with Diet Coke. Out in the countryside, though, when I asked for Diet Coke, I was usually directed to the big Indian brand of cola, Thums Up, which, loaded with sugar, is as far from diet as you can get. I went so far as to download a picture of a Diet Coke can to my phone so that I could use it as a visual aid while trying to feed my caffeine addiction in small roadside mom-and-pop stores. Sometimes even finding a Thums Up on the road was a luxury.

When we drove from Bangalore to Goa, all the way near the west coast, I would have drunk or eaten anything—and I did. I didn't think anything about the three-hundred-mile trip before Vaibhav and I left. That's about how far it is from LA to Vegas, a trip I've made many times before, and we were planning on taking an interstate highway. A piece of cake. The problem turned out to be that for the majority of the drive, large swaths of the highway basically did not exist.

Averaging about 10 miles per hour (any faster than that and our car would have bottomed out on the massive potholes), we passed road crews of women who all looked to be about ninety years old. Holding large, shallow bowls filled with gravel, these ladies were tasked with maintaining the road by hand-sprinkling the gravel. With that kind of crew, I was surprised the roads were in as good shape as they were.

After nine excruciating hours, Vaibhav and I were at the point of starvation. "No problem, sir," our driver said. He knew a great restaurant along the way. In the middle of nowhere, he pulled over at a shack that looked like the perfect place to rob an American and then hack him into little pieces. Inside, the place was absolutely filthy. I could tell that Vaibhav was just as appalled as I was by the grime-caked walls, buzzing flies, and underlying sewer stench. However, neither of us wanted to insult the driver or his friend the cook, who could murder us and take our money. So we settled on an order of eggs, which seemed like the safest bet.

But when the plate of eggs was placed before me, they were covered with ants! The man who ran the place stood over us, wanting to know how we liked his food, while the insects swarmed the runny eggs. I gave him a big American thumbs-up as I shoveled the eggs and ants into my mouth. Luckily we had six more hours of driving for me to digest the special meal.

Panjim, Goa's capital, a beach town located on the Arabian Sea, was a lot more pleasant than the ant omelet, although not without its own perils. We arrived at our bungalow on a beautiful stretch of beach for New Year's 2008 and took the day off from the contest to celebrate. Goa, India's answer to Ibiza, was jam-packed with foreigners. After a long, lazy day on the beach, we spent the night going from club to club, where I was back on my game. I met a cool French chick and was actually able to pick her up, since, unlike the Indian women I had been surrounded by for months, she was definitely not looking to get married. The only unpleasant part of the visit was our mode of transportation: scooter. As we whipped through dicey traffic situations on the little motorized scooters, I was almost killed about twenty times, once even bouncing off the back of a car.

Mostly, however, our trip was about watching kids throw terrible, terrible pitches. Finding potential pitchers turned out to be a lot like fishing. You can go out on a lake and catch a nice, fat fish in the first hour—and then you might not catch anything else for months. During our tour, when a huge range of kids, from those in school uniforms to those without shoes or shirts, gave it their hardest try, sometimes we saw multiple guys who could really bring it in the same day. Other times we went weeks without so much as a nibble.

As I had imagined it would be, the TV show was the bait that on a good day lured as many as a thousand kids to wait in line for their turn on the mound. It wasn't the actual show that aired on TV that provided the attraction; rather, the camera equipment and flat-screen TV playing pitching highlights and a promo for the show had the desired effect of drawing curious kids into our contest. The big setup we hauled all around India was a lot more interesting than *Million Dollar Arm*. If you never saw an episode of the Zee Sports program—well, I would say you're lucky. Even in America, it would be pretty challenging to make an exciting show about of a bunch of guys pitching against a radar gun. But in India, it was downright impossible.

The show's production values were very low, and that is being kind. In 2007 high-definition TV was pretty much nonexistent in most of India. At least two episodes still had the time code used in the editing process of the rough cut when they aired on broadcast TV. *Million Dollar Arm* also never had a specific time slot. It aired simply whenever the last Indian Cricket League match of the day ended. But I didn't go to India to make a great reality show or chase ratings. I went to reach as many potential pitchers as possible, and, in that effort, the show helped immensely. Zee promoted the show across its various platforms, like announcing the dates and places for upcoming qualifiers on Zee News.

No matter how much press we got or how many kids lined up to see if they could light up the radar gun, I wasn't satisfied. I put a tremendous amount of pressure on myself to make the contest succeed. As kid after kid threw only around 50 miles per hour, my stress mounted. Haunted by the thought that I might pass through a town where a potential future Cy Young Award winner lived and never get to see him, I blew my stack every time there was a missed opportunity due to a problem with permits, malfunctioning equipment, or poor turnout.

As the contest wore on without our identifying one truly viable candidate, I started yelling at people for things I would normally let slide. I had so much to supervise, and so much of it was going wrong that I found myself screaming at Vaibhav or the shopkeeper who handed me a Thums Up instead of a Diet Coke, "Can anybody just do their *fucking* job?" My lowest point, though, came when I yelled at some poor kid who just wanted to throw a stupid ball.

In some dusty park in God-knows-where India, this one skinny kid with bangs that brushed his eyes and an arm that had all the strength of a pile of cooked rice lined up over and over again. Each contestant got five throws per turn, but that wasn't enough for this guy, who on his third go-round still hadn't cracked 30 mph. When I saw him approach the mound for a fourth time, I lost it.

"What's wrong with you?" I shouted. "Can't you understand that you are never going to succeed at this no matter how many times you try? You're just doing the same thing over and over. What do you think's going to happen? Miraculously you are going to get some kind of different result? I mean, that is the dictionary definition of futility!

"You are *not* going to succeed here," I went on ranting, "so stop wasting my time, accept defeat, and go home!"

The kid, who might not have understood my tirade but definitely got my meaning, turned away, shamed. It wasn't my finest moment, and of course I was really just projecting my own fears. I had so much at stake with *Million Dollar Arm*. Although there was a significant amount of capital on the line, money wasn't the biggest issue.

More than money, my reputation was on the line. Looking for pitchers in India wasn't like some career study abroad program. As an agent, I had put myself way out on a limb. I had left four extremely high-profile clients back at home to pursue this crazy idea—jeopardizing my relationship with them in the process. For the most part, they were pretty skeptical about my going to India. Barry

Sanders thought I was going to *Indiana* when he first heard the news. That's how out of left field it was for him. Although he didn't say it to my face, I knew that he didn't want his guy halfway around the world. Barry Bonds, after twenty-two years in the bigs, the last fifteen of them as a Giant, was hoping to catch on with another team at the age of forty-three. It was a crucial moment in his career, and he couldn't have been too happy about the timing of my trip. Top athletes aren't going to put up with a six-hour lag in returning their calls due to the time difference, and they aren't going to put up with their business going down.

So I pulled double duty the entire time I was in India. By day, I worked on *Million Dollar Arm,* and then while America was awake, I spent the whole night on the phone. An assistant accompanied my clients to their appearances and shoots, attending to all the details I laid out for her. But I still solicited and booked all the deals and reviewed and signed off on all the contracts.

If I came home empty-handed, it would be a major blow to my judgment, which is the key to being an agent. We had been so sure that we would succeed when everyone else was so sure that we wouldn't. If we didn't, it would be a life of I-told-you-sos. Right now the other side was definitely up.

Well aware that my ability to assess pitching talent was

seriously limited, we'd hired one of the best scouts in the business to look at videotape of the contestants to make sure I hadn't missed anything. (The only baseball player I represented was Barry Bonds, and it doesn't take a genius to figure out he's pretty good; still, if I had seen Barry when he was sixteen years old, I'm not sure I would've known just how good he was.) It takes a special skill to be able to judge talent at the pro level, and that is not a skill that I possess. All I could really do was look at the radar gun. Beyond that, I relied on Ray Poitevint, a man with nearly fifty years of traveling the world to find great players.

Having unearthed talent everywhere from Nicaragua to Korea, Ray believed in the project and agreed to travel to India for the contest finals. For the Baltimore Orioles alone, in the 1970s he discovered and signed first baseman Eddie Murray, a future Hall of Famer, and pitcher Dennis Martínez, who won 245 games in a twenty-three-year MLB career and in 1991 threw a perfect game.

In the meantime, he was back home in Southern California, watching thousands of kids try out on DVD. Ray saw video of every single kid who came anywhere close to hitting 80 miles per hour on the gun.

Mostly, that meant watching tons of kids with absolutely no prayer of becoming baseball players in something akin to a blooper reel. I instructed Ray to call me *immediately* if he saw anyone with a shred of potential that we might have missed. Maybe his eye could detect someone who didn't throw hard but had some easily correctable flaw that might allow for dramatic improvement.

Yet after sending DVDs of thousands of kids, I still hadn't heard one word from Ray.

The morning after I yelled at the kid who took too many turns, I headed out at five in the morning for a run. I found that after a long day of frustration and then an equally long night of working for my American business, I needed to move my body to clear my head and get ready to do it all over again. On this particular morning, I hardly noticed the smoky orange of the sunrise or the coolness of the only fresh air that would exist all day. My mind was racing as fast as my legs with fantasies of failure and embarrassment.

I was about to turn back for my hotel when I crossed paths with a beggar who didn't have any teeth in his head and might have been about 80 years old, although he looked more like 120.

When he spoke, I broke my stride instantly, because I could actually understand his Hindi as he told me, "Don't stop breathing."

CHAPTER 4

By the time we arrived in New Delhi in January to hold a qualifying event, we had it down. Over the course of the contest, we tried out more than thirty-eight thousand young men, which gave us ample opportunity to work out the kinks in the system.

Among the several hundred hopefuls who lined up in yet another dusty park on yet another long, hot day were two friends, Dinesh Kumar Patel and Rinku Singh. Finally, after standing in line for an hour and a half, Rinku stepped up to the cage and held a baseball in his left hand for the first time in his life. The fact that he was a lefty was a good sign: southpaws are always a valuable commodity in baseball because there are relatively few of them to go around. Still, I didn't hold out much hope for anyone, lefty or righty.

Standing six foot two with broad shoulders, Rinku straightened all his limbs and lifted his front leg, so that he looked like a flamingo. His high cheekbones and mouth under his Clark Gable–style mustache were completely stony as he stood perfectly still for so long that I began to wonder if he was actually planning to throw the ball. I had seen a lot of crazy pitching since arriving in India, but this was easily the most bizarre technique I had encountered.

Then in one swift motion, his body uncoiled, and Rinku unleashed a real fastball. The speed from the radar gun flashed on the video monitors: 85 miles per hour! The crowd went crazy. Rinku still didn't crack a smile.

Next up was the right-handed Dinesh, who possessed the same laser-focused intensity as his friend. While most of the other guys were goofing around while on line, hoping to make it on TV, Dinesh didn't even seem to notice the cameras. In fact, he was so serious as he wound up that he looked like he was about to kill someone. With his stocky, powerful five-foot-eleven build, Dinesh was what's known in sports as a fireplug. This was also his first time gripping a baseball. His first pitch registered at 87 miles per hour. The crowd erupted all over again.

Dinesh was, hands down, the best raw pitcher I saw in India. It didn't take a lot of imagination or expertise to understand his ability: he threw harder than anyone else during the course of the tryouts. What made his speed even more impressive was that he did it with terrible mechanics. His right arm swung wildly and long, and his entire torso turned, as if he were throwing a shot put. Nonetheless, he got close to the magic number of 90 mph. Sure, no one knew *where* the ball was headed. But you can teach control; you can't teach how to throw hard. What could this Dinesh kid accomplish if he brought his core and legs into line and got his tempo?

Despite Dinesh's power and speed, it was Rinku who received the highest honor. Out of all the kids that Ray Poitevint watched on video, *only* Rinku prompted him to pick up the phone. "Make sure that lefty with the weird windup is in the finals," Ray said.

Rinku and Dinesh had kept each other company on the twelve-hour train ride from Lucknow, where they attended the same school, to Delhi for the official qualifiers on February 1, 2008. Both of them had traveled even farther than that, however, since they both were raised in small villages worlds away from a big city like Delhi.

In my travels for *Million Dollar Arm*, I had visited a few villages like Rinku's and Dinesh's that dotted India's rural landscape. Many of the thatched-roof houses look like they came straight out of the Middle Ages. The two-story homes seem like a fancier option, until a local explains the second floor is a necessity because flooding renders the ground floor unusable during the rainy-season months.

In some villages, large families cram into one- or two-bedroom homes that don't usually have a door. If they own anything of value, the family will lock it away in a big steel trunk. Most homes in Indian villages also don't have indoor plumbing. There is either an outhouse, or the bathroom is a pit outside. The cooking area—a pipe hooked up to a gas line sticking out of the ground, with some rocks cobbled around it—is outside the house, too. Buffalo mingle with goats that provide thick and nasty milk.

Where Rinku and Dinesh grew up, they didn't have an exact mailing address like in the States or in India's big cities. To send a letter to a village inhabitant, one need put only the person's name, the village name, and the postal code on the envelope. The mailman walks around asking, "Does anybody know where Singh lives?" That's how it works. And bear in mind, probably about 70 percent of the village is named Singh.

The circumstances these guys came from were humble, to say the least. Rinku's father, the devoted head of a family of seven, sacrificed everything in his means to give his children an education. He supported his large brood by driving a vegetable-delivery truck 20 hours a day, 7 days a week, 365 days a year. Like many villagers, the family ate the same dish of rice and dal, a spicy Indian vegetarian stew made out of lentils or beans, for almost every meal, every day. For a special treat, Rinku's father would take part of his wages to buy a chicken from the market. The menu might have been meager in the Singh household, but love and support were certainly in abundance.

Dinesh, whose father did not have a steady source of

income, faced greater economic hardship than Rinku. His mother worked in the fields, growing vegetables to eat and sell, and helped her brother, who ran a silk loom. Dinesh's main motivation was figuring out how to make money to help out his parents and two siblings, whom he loved dearly.

In general, young people in India grow up with a heavy burden of responsibility. A child's primary goal is to ultimately take care of his parents. Only after that has been accomplished can he focus on providing for himself. The need to improve the lot of one's family was instilled in both Dinesh and Rinku.

That was the reason they were enrolled in the Guru Govind Singh Sports College in Lucknow, training in javelin throwing. In India, young athletes attend these government-run academies, the American equivalent of high school, with the implicit aim of competing in the Olympics. India, however, doesn't qualify for nearly enough Olympic events to support all the students at these colleges across the country, so in reality, the colleges are a feeder into coveted jobs in the army, police, or national transportation system.

Rinku and Dinesh became friends when they began training for a spot at Lucknow. They were sixteen when they started to attend. They worked as a team, videotaping each other's tosses and then analyzing the footage together to correct their deliveries. They also traveled together to competitions at other schools.

Javelin throwing explained Rinku's odd pitching motion. When he held his body in that strange pose for a long time before throwing the ball, he was using an adapted version of a javelin training drill called speed packing, in which the athlete throws the javelin parallel to the ground instead of up in the air, to build arm strength. Rinku figured it was the best technique he had to put velocity on a baseball, and he was right. When we conceived *Million Dollar Arm*, I imagined recruiting cricket players, not javelin tossers. But I would have taken someone who skipped stones if he had a good arm.

Rinku and Dinesh threw hard in Delhi, which earned them a trip to the finals. There the best pitcher would win $100,000 and a chance at $1 million. We'd originally planned to fly the top twenty-five contestants from the qualifiers to Mumbai for the finals in March, but, really, there were only a few with any hope of becoming American baseball pitchers, and topping that short list were Rinku and Dinesh.

So when I received the news that they weren't planning on participating in the finals, I almost had a heart attack. I knew the call was going to be bad news as soon as I saw the number on my cell, because it came from an agency employee named Shukla. I dubbed him Crookla, because he was so bad at his job I considered it thievery every time he cashed his paycheck. He was a complete buffoon, a real loser's loser. He screwed up anything I asked him to do— permits, phone numbers, restaurant reservations—or he simply didn't do it at all. Everyone has worked with some-one like this, and it's never fun.

I had asked Shukla to call up all the finalists and make a list of their shoe, pants, and shirt sizes, so that I could buy them clothes for the show. When he called Rinku and Dinesh, that's when both of them told Crookla they couldn't make it to Mumbai.

Before *Million Dollar Arm*, neither Rinku nor Dinesh had ever heard of baseball. Their javelin coach was the one who suggested they try out for the contest in Lucknow in case they could win some money.

Rinku, nineteen, had just finished his fourth and final year at school, and had already set up a recruiting meeting with the army for a month after the *Million Dollar Arm* finals were scheduled to take place. Like most of their classmates, Rinku's and Dinesh's true purpose for school was landing a position in the army that would allow them to earn a salary of about $400 a month—plus a month's vacation each year. That kind of money would vastly improve their families' financial situations.

Rinku's parents did not approve of his traveling all the

way to the big, corrupting city of Mumbai to compete in a contest for this strange sport. What was the point? Even if he won, they opposed him flying to America, an unfathomable prospect, or doing anything else that would jeopardize his military career.

Rinku didn't put up much of a fight, perhaps because he didn't actually believe that *anyone* was really going to win $100,000—much less $1 million. From the beginning, Will, Ash, and I assumed that was the price of entry for producing a reality show. But a $1 million prize had never before been offered on television in India, where the per capita income is less than $1,500. The size of the prize actually damaged our credibility with the ordinary man on the street.

Zee Sports, however, was thrilled about the newsworthy prize and promoted the hell out of it. Apparently, Shahrukh Khan, a very famous Indian actor and host of India's version of *Are You Smarter Than a 5th Grader?*, was livid upon learning that an unheard-of baseball show on a cable sports network was giving away $1 million, when his popular show on a major network was giving away only about $250,000. Shahrukh wound up using us as a negotiating tool to force his network to up its prize by $1 million, for a total of $1.25 million (5 crores).

In my infuriating phone call with Crookla, he told me that some javelin contest with a grand prize of a couple hundred dollars was being held at the academy, and this conflicted with the televised finals of *Million Dollar Arm*. Although Dinesh and Rinku had a chance to win $1 million with us, they were both going with the javelin contest. It was an understatement to say that *Million Dollar Arm* was the opportunity of a lifetime for Rinku and Dinesh. Why would they throw that away for a fraction of that amount?

One day I asked Rinku what he dreamed about becoming when he was a kid. Although I was speaking through an interpreter, since neither he nor Dinesh spoke more than a few words of English at that point, he didn't understand what I meant.

"What did you pretend you were going to be? A cricket player? A fireman?"

"Nahi sapanē," he said in Hindi. "No dreams."

No dreams? There were only about 1,500 people in his village. Its inhabitants all grew up with limited career choices: most would be farmers, or the lucky few got to be in the military or some other government job. Rinku was extremely fortunate to go to the sports college and would be even luckier to get into the military. No one from his village would ever dare dream of becoming a famous writer or a movie star or professional athlete.

I hung up on Crookla without responding. What was the point? All I had left in me were obscenities anyway.

Then I turned to Vaibhav to explain the situation; there was no way I was going to lose the two fastest pitchers out of all the qualifiers all across the country. "You have to fix this."

Vaibhav did what he did best and talked Rinku and Dinesh into changing their minds. He assured them that the contest was real and that they had a legitimate chance of winning. Even if they didn't, they would be in the same exact place with their military careers right after the finals. Rinku said later that the whole contest would have been easier to believe if the grand prize had been just a bunch of prepaid phone cards.

In the last week of March, Dinesh, Rinku, and twenty-three other kids—most of whom had never flown anywhere before—got on a plane to Mumbai for a week of training before the official competition. Over the day or two that all the contestants, scattered throughout India, were traveling, Vaibhav's phone rang every five minutes with the same questions over and over.

"Sir, I am at the counter at the airport; what do I do now?"

"Sir, why will they not let me bring my suitcase on the plane?"

"What is a gate? How do I find which one is mine?"

I was about as familiar with all these different airports as these kids, but I did my best imitation of an air traffic controller and am proud to say that all twenty-five of them wound up safely on the campus of CKT University, right outside of Mumbai. The accommodations were far from cushy. The guys, who ate all their meals in the cafeteria, slept in a big conference room that we'd cleared out and filled with mattresses on the floor. This definitely wasn't the mansion on *The Bachelor*.

Each contestant received a welcome package containing toiletries, sneakers, baseball clothes, and caps— everything he needed for our weeklong crash course in pitching. Vaibhav and I had gone to a big box store called Big Bazaar to buy all the necessary provisions. While I was buying thirty pairs of everything in the Wal-Mart of India, which sold everything from rice to tube socks, I had my first brush with stardom. A couple of gangly teenagers approached me and exclaimed, "Sir, you are *Million Dollar Arm* guy!" They didn't ask for my autograph or anything, but Vaibhav still taunted me, "Look at you, big celebrity!"

The contestants were incredibly excited by everything I got at Big Bazaar. Aside from an aspiring actor and a guy who was working at an investment bank, none of them was wealthy, even by Indian standards, and some were really, really poor. They couldn't believe they had a clean bed (even if they had to share a room with two dozen other guys), three meals a day, and all the Gatorade they could drink. As a contest sponsor, the company provided an ice chest filled with bottles of the sports drink on the field. Although there was more than enough to go around, some kids stashed away bottles back in the dorm. To them, Gatorade was a luxury not to be left on some field.

The bar was low with these guys. This was a good thing, particularly when it came to the uniforms that I had made in India specifically for *Million Dollar Arm*. Just as with all my experiences with manufacturing in India, the factory owner told me, "No problem, sir," after I showed him a picture of a baseball uniform. Well, he wasn't completely wrong. The way he made the shirts was no problem—for him. When I opened up the boxes of shirts, which, of course, came at the very last minute possible the day of the contest, I could not believe my eyes. At first I thought Vaibhav was playing a joke on me. The manufacturer had taken all my instructions—what the seams should look like, where the buttons went—but instead of sewing the seams and putting buttons on the shirt, he had simply printed all those details as a design on the shirt. They looked utterly ridiculous, like tuxedo T-shirts, but they were our uniforms.

Ray Poitevint arrived in India to train our guys. As one of the most successful scouts in history, Ray has a sixth sense about it. Talent is not just what a radar gun says; it is what a baseball player looks like, feels like, and even sounds like. That's right: Ray could close his eyes and *hear* a good pitcher by the sound of the ball cutting the air.

He has opened up a lot of foreign markets to baseball, but no matter where Ray has gone to "eat mama's meatloaf" (a term among agents for whatever unusual local cuisine you have to sample when you're recruiting a player), he is the same guy. In India, though, he didn't quite take to *paneer,* a type of cheese, as well as he might have, say, meatloaf. When on the first day I saw him looking kind of uncomfortable, I asked if he was okay. "It's just that green stuff I ate last night," he said.

That wasn't the last of Ray's trials. Obviously, there was no baseball diamond available at the university, so we set up on a wide, open dirt field in the middle of the campus. Our only protection from the brutally hot sun was a tent, under which it was even hotter. That was the seventy-four-year-old scout's base.

The focus of his pointers was to maximize their velocity and control. A week obviously wasn't a lot of time, and we were starting from the ground up with every one of these kids, but Ray was a very effective teacher. He demonstrated how to start the pitch by lifting the front leg and some basic ways to grip the ball. He had them on the field doing long tosses and throwing from one knee, standard drills that pitchers use to get loose and improve their technique.

I had also gotten the Wilson Sporting Goods Company to sponsor the event and give us all these brand-new gloves, but none of the contestants wanted to use them. Staring at them as if a strange creature had perched on their hand and wouldn't get off, the Indian kids wanted to take off the mitts and play bare-handed. One of our major priorities, however, was making sure that no one got hurt. With twenty-five kids who had hardly thrown a baseball before spending a week throwing it as hard as they could, that wasn't easy. Without the mitts, and with guys who couldn't toss the ball without whaling it, fielding without a glove was downright dangerous.

On the field, our contestants dropped so many balls, Ray said sarcastically, "Maybe we *should* just let them catch bare-handed."

That was just Ray being Ray. He really sparked to how respectful the kids were and how hard they worked. Compared with the generally immature and often spoiled American youth that he usually coached, these kids were extremely respectful—particularly since Ray was a man of a certain age. They were quiet when he talked, asked questions about what they heard, and worked hard on the drills he offered them. They understood that he was try-ing to help them do the best they could do in the contest, and in return, they did the best they could for him.

By the second or third day, though, it was clear that a couple of kids had no chance. We had seen all kinds of crazy deliveries throughout the contest. Usually the people with really bad form didn't get anything on the ball. However, among the contestants we brought to Mumbai, one guy from Goa managed to top 80 miles per hour on the radar gun throwing almost underhand like submarine-style pitchers Dan Quisenberry and Kent Tekulve. Then there was a kid who somehow made the finals even though he released the ball from right next to his face, as if it were a shot put.

The kid who won the contest for showing the most heart was Deepak Kundal, but he couldn't throw 90 miles an hour in a car that was going 91. He knew he had no prayer of winning, and yet he was on time every day. He paid attention. He tried as hard as he could in every drill, every day.

Just as devoted, if not more, to this foreign sport and these strange American men was Ray's translator, Deepesh Solanki. A college athletic coach in his twenties, he sought us out as soon as he heard about *Million Dollar Arm*. He sent me an email, he sent Ash an email; he basically stalked us, begging to be a part of our contest in any way.

Deepesh was without a doubt the most passionate baseball fan I had ever met in India. Of course, he was the *only* baseball fan in India I met. He fell in love after discovering the sport on the internet. The field, the uniforms, the strategy—he found everything about the game beautiful. He even played baseball in college. Other than a Little League run by Joel Ehrendreich, an ardent Milwaukee Brewers fan and an assistant to the American ambassador, on embassy grounds, Deepesh's team played, to the best of my knowledge, the only other organized baseball in all of India. Most other "baseball" teams were really softball teams scattered through some major cities.

I made Deepesh's dreams come true when I put him in charge of making the arrangements for the training camp and the finals. To be honest, I had no idea whether he was actually capable of pulling it off. By that point in my great Indian adventure, I had stopped trying to make that assessment. In this country, I had found the people who were supposed to be the most professional were the ones who ripped me off the most. And the people who seemed like they couldn't do anything were the ones who wound up getting things done.

When I first arrived in India, something called the Baseball Federation of India contacted us about teaming up with its organization to bring contestants to our events. It seemed like a natural partnership. We had meeting after meeting after meeting, the result of which was an agreement that it would bring three thousand kids to a qualifier in Punjab. I was thrilled—until the day of the contest. The federation brought a total of seven kids. *Seven kids.* The craziest part was that a representative from the organization came with them and asked us to give them money to develop baseball in India or for equipment that they would probably sell on the black market. I don't know the Hindi word for chutzpah, but they had it in spades.

Deepesh might have followed me around like a puppy dog and startled easily, but I knew two things about him: he worked for CKT University and loved baseball. He coached youth athletics at the university in a remote area outside of Mumbai, which is just where I wanted my guys. I didn't want them out in the city, getting into trouble or not coming back.

He did everything he said he would—setting up all aspects of the stay at CKT, from locating the mattresses for our makeshift dorm to getting enough dal for all the guys to eat—so that leading up to the day of the finals, March 21, 2007, I couldn't have felt better about my decision to trust him.

I also felt pretty good on the day of the finals. Walking out of my hotel in a crisp white *Million Dollar Arm* shirt, I felt like a million bucks. I was excited about the possibility of finally proving the thesis that Ash, Will, and I had developed in Will's San Mateo office: that there were guys walking around India who could throw a baseball and simply didn't know it. I was happily thinking about how we had gone with the goal of finding just one guy, and now it looked like we had at least two, when suddenly an explosion of powder stung my face.

Was it a terrorist attack? A rabid cricket fan getting me back for encroaching on the sport's dominance by introducing a little baseball?

As I cleared the fine powder from my eyes, a bunch of laughing kids came into focus. Red, blue, and green rained down from my head, only causing them to laugh even harder. It turned out that the brightly colored powder was part of the Hindu holiday celebrating the start of spring. For *Holi*, or the Festival of Colors, kids run around the street pelting everyone with rainbow-colored powder as part of the celebration. So much for my white shirt.

Despite the fact that I had been completely cropdusted, I was still eager to see how the finals played out. According to the rules we set up, every contestant would be allowed to throw twenty pitches. Whoever threw the most strikes over 85 miles per hour would be crowned the winner and awarded $100,000. Then the winner would get to throw three more pitches for the chance to win the $1 million prize. He would win $250,000 for throwing one strike at 90 miles per hour, and $500,000 for throwing two consecutively. If the winner by some miracle managed to throw three consecutive 90 mph strikes, the grand total of $1 million was his.

Dinesh was up first. Nobody could throw 90-mile-per-hour pitches like him. My heart beat loudly as he took the pitcher's mound, wound up, and whipped the ball. It sped through the air and hit the hand of the mannequin we had set up in the batter's box as a hitter, shattering the plastic. Dinesh took a deep breath and then threw five or six pitches that, although they clocked in right around 90 mph, came nowhere close to hitting the strike zone. His last pitch went behind the batting mannequin's head, snapping off the barrel of the bat it was holding. We hadn't prepared for that. There was no backup mannequin to come in off the bench, and, as they say, the show must go on. So Deepesh ran like the wind and returned with duct tape, which we used to put our batter back together.

Dinesh wasn't known for his fine placement of the ball, but his turn during the finals had been a little wild, even for him. The contest went on, and one by one, our finalists all got up in front of the cameras and failed to throw a single strike over 85 miles per hour.

With each pitch that seemed to miss the strike zone by about a mile, my anxiety spiked another level. We were looking for speed *and* accuracy in deciding whom to bring back to America. But most of the contestants were concerned mostly with speed, so they threw as hard as they possibly could, with little regard for accuracy.

From training camp, I knew that at least some of the guys had the raw ability to get strikes over 90 mph. But as any athlete or fan knows, there's a big difference between doing things in practice and doing them when the pressure is on. The contestants were keenly aware of not only how much money was at stake but also how many people were watching them on TV.

When the twentieth guy flunked out, my jitters started to get the better of me, too. Technically, we didn't *have* to have a winner or give away a $100,000 prize. But we'd been touring the country for months and months on this premise. Someone *had* to win the money and get rich on our TV show, or we would look like fools at best and charlatans at worst.

With only four pitchers left, Rinku took the mound. I laughed nervously at the tai chi–like style he still hadn't completely abandoned. His first pitch was wild, sending my heart down into my stomach. *Come on, Rinku!* His second came dangerously close to the poor batter's rigged hand. Then he did it: the Flamingo Kid threw a strike that clocked in at 87 mph!

We sat through the last three contestants, which was practically a formality, and then as soon as they were through, everyone jumped all over Rinku as if he had just pitched a perfect game to win the World Series. There wasn't a sore loser in the bunch as the rest of the guys hoisted him high up on their shoulders. Then Rinku received what may well have been the first Gatorade shower in the history of

India. He looked as alarmed by the unfamiliar ritual of getting doused by juice as I had been by the *Holi* color war. But the contest wasn't over yet. In his soaked uniform, Rinku still had to try to win the $1 million.

There was almost no chance that Rinku would win the grand prize, because there was basically no chance that *anyone* could win it. When I ran into pitching great Roger Clemens at a celebrity golf tournament in America, way before the finals, he told me that even he wouldn't have been able to win the $1 million given the way we set it up. Natural ability without extensive training (we're talking years, not a week) only goes so far. Generating that kind of velocity and accuracy is next to impossible for someone lacking that training. Clemens estimated that the winner would be lucky if he could throw one strike.

So when we looked into insuring the $1 million in the rare event that someone did win it, and the quotes came back ridiculously high, we decided to take our chances. Will wasn't eager to shell $1 million out of his own pocket. By the same token, if we found a kid who was able to consistently throw 90-mile-per-hour strikes after a week of training with Ray, $1 million would be a small price to pay for such a rare talent. He'd make back that money for us and a lot more when he signed a pro contract.

Despite all the evidence before me, I did hold my breath as Rinku took the mound for a second time. Not only was he soaking wet; he was also drained emotionally. It had been a long mental and physical road: disobeying his parents in making the trip to Mumbai, giving it his all for an intensive week of training in a sport that was completely new to him, and maintaining his composure to win $100,000—on TV. Then to hand him a ball and ask him to throw one, two, or three strikes at 90 mph? He didn't come close.

One hundred thousand dollars was still an enormous sum for Indian TV—and even larger for a kid from a tiny village in the north Indian state of Uttar Pradesh. It was more than enough to transform the lives of his entire family.

Almost as soon as he came off the mound, Rinku wanted to call home to share the news of their new fortune. But first he had to tell his parents where he was and what he had done. They still thought that he was in Lucknow at a javelin-throwing contest. After confessing that he had betrayed their wishes by going to Mumbai, he proudly informed his father that he was now retired, effective immediately. Now that his son was able to take care of him, it was finally time for his father to relax and enjoy his life. As proud as Rinku might have felt, Ash and I were equally elated. There have never been two people happier to part with $100K than Ash and I were at that moment.

* * *

Though the contest was over, my work was just beginning. We had three finalists—Rinku, Dinesh, and an impressive sixteen-year-old named Manoj Shukla—all of whom we decided to bring back to the States for training. (Since no one but Rinku threw a strike over 85 miles per hour, we ranked everyone else based strictly on velocity.) Manoj, one of the youngest in the entire contest, probably had the most raw talent of all three. Although he was very skinny, to the point of undernourished, the six-foot-two teenager was still able to throw around 85 mph right off the bat, with a little bit of control.

During the finals in Mumbai, he was not nearly as serious as Rinku and Dinesh. A class-clown type, he was always showing up late to meetings and then making jokes in Hindi that made everyone laugh—and, I'm sure, were at my expense. Manoj was also in love, listening constantly to romantic Hindi songs on his cell phone. But he was a sixteen-year-old boy—one who, if given the right diet and training, could become a legitimate prospect for the major leagues.

The problem with Manoj wasn't his attitude. Rather, it was getting him a passport. As I entered the bureaucratic morass of visas and passports for our three winners, which made getting the permits seem like child's play, I quickly found myself facing the most unexpected and devastating by-product of poverty. Because he and his family came from one of India's many slums, where people lived in temporary housing and survived by carrying packages, running errands, picking through trash, or begging, there was no official record of his existence.

Manoj's parents didn't pay rent or taxes. They didn't have jobs with IDs or pay stubs. He wasn't enrolled in school. No one in his family had a state-issued identification card or any way to get one. Manoj, who had been born in whatever his family called home at the time and not a hospital, didn't have a birth certificate.

For six weeks, I tried everything I could think of, and Vaibhav talked his way through every official, but to no avail. To make matters worse, without our knowing, Manoj had given what little money his family could muster to a con artist who'd promised him identification documents. Still, I refused to give up hope. I was determined to find a way for Manoj to join us, and in the meantime found him a baseball coach and living situation so that he could continue to train in Mumbai while we trained in the States.

Ultimately, even though Manoj had lived in India his whole life, we didn't know how to prove that he was a citizen. And with that, his chance to visit the United States—and possibly to transform his and his family's futures—flickered out.

CHAPTER 5

I startled awake to someone shaking my shoulder. It was Dinesh, his serious brow furrowed more deeply than usual. "Sir, big problem."

I was more than aware of the enormous responsibility of taking a few sheltered Indian kids, who hadn't even been out of their region, let alone out of their country, and bringing them to the United States, where the opportunities for personal advancement and personal corruption were equally great. But we hadn't even landed yet. In fact, we were only about a third of the way through our flight to America when Dinesh came up from coach to find me in business class. (I was an old man and couldn't sit for sixteen hours in coach. Meanwhile, they were more than fine in those seats, amazed at the televisions built into the headrests in front of them.) Something was wrong already?

Even though we had to bridge a language gap the size of the Indian Ocean, I could tell that he was very embarrassed without him saying a word. But Deepesh was on hand to translate.

Throughout the finals, Deepesh never suspected in a

million years that he would be coming to America. But, despite the fact that Rinku's and Dinesh's English, which was nonexistent when I met them, was improving every day, I knew they would still need help communicating with the coaches and other players in America. While he was in the States, not only would Deepesh work with Rinku and Dinesh, but I planned for him to become NCAA certified as both a coach and an umpire. With those credentials, he could return to India after Rinku's and Dinesh's training was over and become the go-to resource for baseball in his native country. When I offered him the job after the finals, he almost had a heart attack.

Deepesh translated that Dinesh had left the airplane toilet without flushing. I saw the boy's cheeks redden beneath his caramel-colored complexion. He hadn't been able to find a handle to flush—because there was no handle, just a button.

Good grief. We were really starting at zero here. Flustered and nervous, Dinesh had decided that the best thing to do was leave the bathroom door open and find me. I'm sure the next guy in line took care of the situation, but I went back to where he and Rinku were sitting to have a stewardess give a demonstration of the button that flushes the toilet. For future reference.

Looking at Rinku, Dinesh, and Deepesh in their seats, I keenly felt Manoj's absence, and the old anger at my failure to get him a passport rose up again. Even for Rinku and Dinesh, the Indian consular system had been merciless. When we found ourselves waiting on yet another endless line for visas the day before our flight to the States, I tried to hurry things along by explaining the unusual circumstances to the expressionless bureaucrats.

"These guys are attempting to become the first Indian athletes to ever go pro in a major American sport," I said. "But they have to leave tomorrow!" The people at the Indian embassy couldn't have cared less.

"Please, sir. Step back in line, sir."

As tough as the Indian visa process was, the US visa process was the direct opposite. We were whisked through our security check at the American embassy, and the boys' passports were processed while Assistant to the Ambassador Joel Ehrendreich took us on a tour of the grounds. Less than an hour later, the boys were the guests of the ambassador, David Mulford, at his personal residence for a press conference to give them their visas and to wish them luck. The ambassador, gracious in his speech that emphasized the importance of sports as a tool in diplomacy, hoped that the boys' endeavor would create yet another link in the strong bond between India and the United States. Joel's son and a friend each played catcher for Rinku and Dinesh in the ambassador's yard as they gave a brief pitching demonstration. The ambassador even rolled up his sleeves and threw a few. After waiting a month for their Indian passports, we got their US visas and a press conference completed in less than two hours. It was an amazing moment and reminded us of the historical nature of what the boys were about to attempt.

We made it, through the visa process and the flight, landing on May 3, 2008, in Los Angeles. There we planned to spend six months getting Rinku and Dinesh ready for the Major League Baseball tryouts.

From the moment we arrived, everything around them was different from what they were used to. They were even in disbelief during the ride from the airport to their hotel.

"Where are all the three-wheelers?" Rinku wanted to know, referring to the auto rickshaws that were basically glorified golf carts used all over India to shuttle people around.

"It's so quiet!" Dinesh commented.

Back home, everybody honked the horn all the time, even when twenty-four-hour gridlock traffic made it an absurd cacophony.

"And clean!" Rinku added.

They marveled at how all the cars stayed in their lanes and how smooth the road felt.

"But, sir," Dinesh asked. "How is it that every car in America is new?"

Compared to the three-wheelers and ancient trucks that clogged the roads in India, all the cars outside the window looked like high-end luxury vehicles.

Naturally, the first thing they both wanted to do was to call home and let their parents know they had arrived safely. I handed my cell phone to Rinku, who dialed his number and joyfully said hello to whichever parent answered. Soon, however, the conversation clearly turned into an argument. I heard him repeat the Hindi words for sun, *suraj,* and moon, *chandni,* with frustration while jabbing his index finger at the window.

It seemed that neither Rinku nor his parents could reconcile the fact that although it was night where he was at that very moment, it was daytime back in India. Both thought the other party was playing an annoying joke. At the first opportunity I had, I pulled out a tennis ball and a flashlight to explain the rotation of the earth and how that means only half the planet is lit by the sun at any given time. First how to flush an airplane toilet and now basic astronomy; it looked like I was going to have to introduce the boys to a lot more than baseball.

To start off their first day in the States, I decided to give them an education in American diner food by taking them to breakfast at Denny's. I chose the chain and its Grand Slam breakfast because the menu had pictures of the food. Having settled into a booth, the boys studied the bright laminated pictures of crinkly bacon, eggs with bright yellow yolks, pancakes topped by a scoop of butter, and steaming coffee. When the waitress came to take their orders, I was surprised that they both pointed to the image depicting a T-bone steak flanked by fried eggs and hash browns. Steak and eggs?

Beef was totally taboo in many parts of India, since cows are considered sacred in Hinduism. In many states in India, slaughtering cows is against the law. It's not just gross, like eating a pet; it's a sin.

I thought about saying something and then thought again. If I were a teenager and away from home in a different country for the first time, the first thing I might do is order a steak to see what all the fuss was about. My job was not to be the theological police but to help them become great pitchers—and they both definitely needed to up their protein intake.

As soon as the waitress delivered their orders of steak and eggs, two plates so heaped with food that Dinesh lifted the plate to see how much it weighed, they dug in with the ferocious appetite universal to all male teenagers. Now, these were Denny's steaks—certainly not the choicest cuts of meat—but both of them were pouring A1 steak sauce all over the food and enjoying themselves immensely.

About halfway through the meal, as both boys began

to slow down a little, Rinku asked me, "What part of the chicken is this?"

Oh Lord. They had never seen a steak, so they had no idea what it was. They thought it was some exotic part of the chicken we had only here in America. I thought they lived on a farm. How did they confuse this for chicken? All I knew was that I had to break some very bad news. I went with the straightforward approach, since it's the only one I know.

"*Gaya*," I said, using the Hindi word for cow.

Rinku did a double take.

"*Gaya?*"

I nodded, and his face went white. He slowly stopped working the piece he had been chewing and forced it down his throat.

Dinesh, looking up from his plate, repeated the question: "*Gaya?*"

Again, I nodded yes.

"It's good," he said, continuing to saw away with his knife and fork without guilt.

Rinku and Dinesh might have reacted to the incident in different ways, but neither was so traumatized by the true source of the meat on his plate that it ruined his appetite for the many, many snacks they sampled to great delight at the baseball game I took them to later that day.

It seemed only natural that Rinku and Dinesh should

spend their first day in America taking in a baseball game. The college matchup of the University of Washington Huskies versus the University of Southern California Trojans was not only the first time either of them got to watch the sport that they were about to attempt to play professionally. It was also the first live professional sporting event they had been to in their lives.

They were filled with questions before the top of the first inning. It was a perfect day, not a cloud to be seen. The stadium was about three-quarters full, and we were sitting fifteen rows up and to the left of home plate. The sights, sounds, and smells Americans take for granted at a baseball game—fresh-cut grass, fried foods, the crisp uniforms on the players—were all new to them. They thought the field was beautiful—the greenest grass they ever saw. As USC's first baseman threw grounders to the other infielders while the pitcher warmed up, Dinesh pointed to the shortstop and asked me what he did wrong.

"Nobody did anything wrong," I told him. "The game hasn't even started yet."

But Dinesh was insistent. When I pressed him about why he thought the shortstop was in trouble, Dinesh, pointing to the third baseman standing next to the third base bag, said, "He has a square." The second baseman had a square; so did the first baseman. The pitcher had a mountain, and the guy in the armor (the catcher) had a pentagon (also known as home plate). But the shortstop? What did he have? Nothing.

Where could I even begin?

I decided to distract him by calling over the Cracker Jack vendor. Indians typically enjoy snack foods such as spicy nut and rice mixes, but Rinku and Dinesh gobbled up the candy-coated popcorn and peanuts. I had to buy another box quickly; otherwise I thought they were going to come to fisticuffs over the last handful. That was just the start of their gastronomical tour of Dedeaux Field, the USC ballpark. They sampled French fries, real Coke (Thums Up rightly got a big thumbs-down by comparison), and the pièce de résistance: nachos. They ate so many of the chips slathered in the taxicab yellow cheese that I was scared they were going to develop sodium poisoning.

When they were able to tear themselves away from the food, they marveled at the high level of every part of the game being played: the pristinely manicured green grass of the field, the bright white of the uniforms, the excited chants from the crowd, the *thwack!* of the aluminum bat hitting the ball, the smoothness of the plays, and, of course, the speed of the pitches.

I hoped that the most trouble the guys would get into was a stomachache from indigestion, particularly as I had set them up with their own room at the Radisson hotel right by USC, where they would be training. Even though the first five floors of the hotel are actually USC dorm rooms, Dinesh and Rinku found a way to get on the nerves of the other people staying there. They didn't do anything typical of an American college student, like passing out drunk in the hallway or in somebody else's room. The boys were so blown away by the motion sensor in the elevator that they took any opportunity to see it in action. (They were also amazed by escalators; Rinku in particular didn't understand who could be so lazy that they needed moving stairs.)

Rinku and Dinesh called the elevator even when they had nowhere to go. Once inside, they waved their hands right before the doors closed so that they popped back open. This delighted them to the point that they didn't care if they held up other guests. And if someone else happened to step into the elevator, that didn't stop them. Demonstrating the sensor for the new arrivals, Rinku said, "See, this magic!"

That wasn't the only way they made their presence known. They knew that they had to use every waking minute of the following year to become baseball players if they were going to have a shot at the major leagues, and they wasted no time getting started. In their room, they practiced the towel drill: where one person holds an open glove in front of him while the other, who has a baseball wrapped up in the end of a towel, goes through his pitching motion, trying to smack the towel into the other guy's glove.

In order to hit the glove consistently, the guy with the ball needs to replicate the exact same motion over and over, which is one of the keys to being a successful pitcher. So all night long, a strange, loud, and annoying smacking noise came from their room. *Whap! Whap! Whap!* They barely ever slept, because they were that committed to their goal. (When they weren't running baseball drills, they were calling home. Having found a loophole that allowed them to make two minutes of free phone calls on Skype when you opened a new account, they must have set up a hundred new Gmail accounts for the free minutes.) As a result, the hotel staff wasn't sorry to say goodbye when the beautiful mansion that Ash had found for us right on the USC campus was ready for us to move into.

The word "mansion" doesn't do this place justice. This was more than a house; it was a historical monument. Built back in 1890, it had five sprawling bedrooms and an attic that we turned into our personal film room. But the coolest part of the house was its secret passageways. Just like in those old mystery movies, there was a bookcase on a wall with a certain book that if pulled spun the bookcase around and led to a hallway that dead-ended in a wine rack. Except that it wasn't really a dead end. On one of the bottles there was a button, which if pressed sent another secret door sliding open to reveal a whole downstairs area. It was wild. I had no idea what it was for; maybe a secret party room back during Prohibition? But we turned it into a home gym.

There are very few houses like this in America—or the world, for that matter. For Rinku and Dinesh, used to one-room houses where entire families slept together, it was truly unbelievable. They were in shock that each of them had his own bedroom *and* bathroom! They walked around checking out every single aspect of the place, staring openmouthed at the giant plasma TV, turning on the water from the rain showerhead, reclining in the overstuffed armchairs, touching the soft green lawn, and smelling the bright pink roses.

And just like that, I inherited a ready-made family of three Indians.

Deepesh didn't just translate but also acted as a chaperone. Although he wasn't more than five years older than the boys, Deepesh was a natural babysitter. That's because he took his role and everything I demanded of it seriously. Maybe a little too seriously.

After handing Deepesh a copy of *Baseball for Dummies*, with the instruction to quiz the guys on game situations (If a ball is hit to left field with a runner on first, where do you throw?), he held nightly tests that often went well into the wee hours—and by all accounts got pretty animated.

I could always count on Deepesh dotting all the i's and crossing the t's. He did exactly what I asked, and I mean exactly. When he arrived in the United States, I gave him a video camera and told him that one of his jobs was to video everything Rinku and Dinesh did. A couple of weeks into their stay, when I went to look at some of Deepesh's footage, I discovered hours and hours of Rinku and Dinesh walking in the rose garden at USC, deciding what to have for lunch, eating Chinese food for said lunch, sitting in a hot tub to relax their sore muscles, and even watching TV. When I asked him why there was all this random footage on the camera, he got flustered: "You said to videotape everything, sir. That is what I am doing. I am videoing everything." I had meant that he should video everything they did for their pitching, not *everything*.

I had to be very careful with my words around Deepesh, and not just because of his literal interpretations of my instructions. A dedicated worker, Deepesh lived in fear of disappointing me. His biggest worry was being yelled at—a fact that Rinku and Dinesh used to tease the crap out of him.

"Sir, please do it," Rinku pleaded while we were watching TV downstairs.

"Oh, come on."

"Sir, please!" Dinesh whined.

"Please," they both begged.

I rolled my eyes and then yelled at the top of my lungs, *"Deepesh, get down here!"*

With papers flying, Deepesh came careening from his room where he was working, practically killing himself on the stairs. When he was in front of us on the couch, panting and, of course, flustered, he said, "Sir, sir, what's the matter?"

The boys broke out in hysterics.

"Why are you doing this to me, sir? You are making me so scared that something is very, very wrong."

Rinku and Dinesh made me pull this prank over and over, and each time it worked, because Deepesh never could be sure it was truly a joke. I was sorry that Deepesh had to add "fall guy" to his job description, but with all that Rinku and Dinesh were dealing with, I couldn't begrudge them letting off a little steam.

It wasn't just having to contend with the herculean task of learning baseball in six months. Every single thing was new, and even the littlest element of American life—stuff that I took for granted as ordinary—was extraordinary to them.

The first night in the new house, when I was trying to decide what we should have for dinner, Dinesh asked, "Sir, pizza possible, sir?" Possible? Pizza was always possible! I ordered three large pies so that they could try pepperoni, veggie, and plain. When the bell rang forty minutes later, Dinesh was the one to answer the door.

"Sir," he said excitedly, having run back in to find me, "it's the pizza god!"

No. It was just the pizza delivery guy.

Dinesh addressed the kid holding the pizza: "Sir, how you knowing what we want?"

The surly teenager looked at Dinesh like he was a freak. I handed him the money, took the pizza, and closed the doors.

Over the pies that the boys demolished, Dinesh was full of questions. Although McDonald's delivered in some Indian cities, food delivery was unheard of in the villages, where even the presence of a restaurant was rare. Dinesh puzzled over how the man, if he wasn't the god of pizza, knew not only that we wanted pizza but also where we lived.

I solved for them the mystery of food delivery, but food in general—the quantity of choices and portion size—continued to be a major point of amazement for two boys used to a steady, daily diet of dal. The first time Rinku and Dinesh experienced the USC food court, they walked around in a daze of abundance. As they circled the space over and over, they couldn't believe that a single area had thirty different restaurants to choose from. Pizza, burgers, salads, pastries, overstuffed deli sandwiches, falafel, burritos, tacos, ramen, doughnuts, chips—foods that they had never seen or even knew existed. Eventually they responded to the Chinese food counter's sign to "Wok on over!" where they ordered the number 13: chicken fried rice. They happily shoveled the mountain of greasy rice dotted with dark pieces of chicken and green peas into their mouths. Despite all the choices at their disposal, they ordered the number 13 every time they ate at the food court, which was a lot, so that after a while, the girl at the counter started plating it up as soon as she saw them coming.

While the four of us certainly ate out our fair share, I also insisted they learn how to cook. I considered their time in the kitchen part of their training to become baseball players. If they were going to enter minor-league baseball, they were going to need to know how to take care of themselves in every way. I had seen the life up close, and it was far from glamorous and very unforgiving. To prepare them, I turned into a drill sergeant, demanding self-reliance and orderliness. I knew that most of the coaches in organized baseball were old school and didn't consider it their job to be a nanny, chef, or life coach. Many pro sports, in fact, view athletes more as investments than as people.

So I set about teaching Rinku and Dinesh how to cook. But I was no Julia Child. Before the guys came to live with me, I hadn't cooked a meal in about a decade. My diet consisted of nothing for breakfast, a sandwich grabbed on the go for lunch, and takeout for dinner. As far as I was concerned, the fridge was simply a large Diet Coke cooler.

Now I was like a soccer mom, walking the supermarket aisles nearly every other day, because those kids went through food like you wouldn't believe. I'd load up on groceries, fretting that the cupboards would be bare when they came home from practice for lunch, and restocking their favorites—including ice cream, which rivaled their passion for fried rice.

Meals in our little household were not beef Wellington and coq au vin. We ate a lot of sandwiches and eggs. Not that Rinku and Dinesh lacked for enthusiasm when it came to preparing food. One night when I was out of town, they decided to barbecue chicken for a friend I'd asked to come over and check on them. After pouring a bottle of sauce over a whole raw chicken, lighting the grill only partially, so that the whole backyard smelled of gas, and then putting the bird on the fire for about eight seconds, they proudly plated up their barely warm barbecued salmonella.

Their skills were much better suited to breakfast, where they perfected the art of the pancake. I had taught them how to make pancakes—meaning that I showed them a box of Bisquick and a pan. Pancakes quickly became a favorite, and the boys made them over and over. One morning, they wondered what it would be like if they filled the whole pan with batter.

"Sir! Sir!" they shouted from the kitchen. I rushed in, thinking that they had finally set themselves or the house on fire.

"Sir, supercake, sir!"

Rinku slapped a pancake the size of a garbage can lid on a plate so that it flopped over on all sides and handed it to me.

"This is good supercake," he enthused.

He was right! The supercake with caramelized banana on the bottom was good and became a staple of our lives.

Rinku and Dinesh were certainly a lot better at cooking than at cleaning. Obviously, I could have hired someone to clean the place, but I wanted the guys to learn responsibility. I put them in charge of cleaning the bathrooms; each was handed a bottle of Clorox spray bleach and was instructed to use it once a week to clean the showers, sinks, and floors.

About a week later, I was doing the laundry when I noticed that all of my towels were covered with bleach spots. I assumed that I'd accidentally added bleach to the wash, although that was very unlike me. Over the many years I'd been living as a bachelor, I'd become a pretty fastidious housekeeper. But it kept happening. I finally put two and two together and asked the guys to show me how they cleaned the bathrooms. After drying off from the shower, they sprayed the Clorox and then used their towel to wipe down the shower. Then they replaced the towel on the rack to dry and use it again the next day for a shower and Clorox scrub! I had neglected to mention the need to use cleaning rags, so they had turned every single towel I owned into a cleaning rag.

Some of the discrepancies in our notions of proper hygiene were cultural. I had trouble selling Rinku on the concept of a garbage bag. He thought I was absolutely out of my mind to pay good money to buy a brand-new plastic bag for the sheer purpose of filling it up with garbage and throwing it away. Where he came from in India, everyone piled his trash on a street corner, where it would sit for a week, attracting flies and who knows what else, until it was shoveled into a truck. To me, that wasn't only crazy but revolting.

A number of our differences had just as much to do with the fact that, nearing my forties and used to living alone, I was now living with two teenage boys.

"I am an extremely neat person," I said as a cautionary note when they moved in.

"Sir, I am very tidy," Dinesh assured me.

Not to me, he wasn't.

I took orderliness to another level; everything had a designated place, and nothing could be out of place ever. The TV remotes should be lined up on the left corner of the coffee table. The magazines should be fanned out on the side table by the recliner. And the dishes should be in the kitchen cupboards—put away, clean.

It was a constant struggle getting Dinesh and Rinku to pick up after themselves. For two young guys learning to play ball all day, tidying up just wasn't a priority. But when I discovered bowls with cruddy Cheerios decaying in milk in the sink all day, it was like nails on a chalkboard. Same with a towel on the floor or draped over an upholstered chair instead of on the towel rack. And leaving the sheets and blanket all crumpled up at the end of the bed? Really?

I mean, is it so hard when you are done brushing your teeth to rinse the gunk from the side of the sink? The answer is no; all it takes is a few splashes of water.

Reduced to a nag, I constantly cajoled the guys to clean their dirty dishes, hang up the towels, and make the bed.

"It only takes thirty seconds to pull the covers up," I implored. "I'm not talking about a military inspection. I'm not going to bounce a quarter."

I knew it was slightly irrational bugging these two exhausted kids who were a million miles and worlds away from home about making their beds. But I was so set in my ways that not doing things my way seemed even crazier than bothering them about it. I couldn't help but put their clothes away in their closets. Anything else was uncomfortable for me.

In spite of it all, we quickly found a domestic groove that collectively began around six o'clock when they got up and did their morning rituals of yoga and meditation. (I was already up, because I am up all the time.) Over one of the fireplaces in our house, they hung banners for the Hindu gods Ganpati and Shiva and arranged a couple of small statues into a little shrine. Whatever it took to get them going. While they prayed and stretched, I wrote emails.

Rinku and Dinesh found other ways to decompress during the day. We set up a garden outside, where they liked to relax by watering the flowers. They also unwound by watching a lot of TV. They were in awe of the plasma and how real—better than real—everything looked. And the surround sound nearly made them flinch. We watched a ton of movies; they couldn't get enough of American action flicks and Westerns.

The more gore and violence the better, except when it came to sports. Rinku and Dinesh weren't big fans of American football. When they saw firsthand the brutality of the sport, they were both very thankful they had won a baseball contest instead. "I could not take a hitting once,"

Rinku said. Mostly, though, we watched a lot of baseball, and the guys started to follow certain pitchers. Rinku was a fan of Cliff Lee, a star left-hander for the Cleveland Indians, while Dinesh liked Lee's teammate C. C. Sabathia, another southpaw.

At the time, Viagra, a big sponsor of MLB, aired its "Viva Viagra" campaign incessantly. The guys, who were already jingle enthusiasts, really took to the theme song—Elvis Presley's "Viva Las Vegas" but with different words—singing it *all the time.* I let it go for a while, but, worrying that they might start singing it in the USC food court, I decided I had to tell them exactly what the ad was selling. I knew they had no clue; the commercial was far from obvious. There was some guy square dancing, another riding a motorcycle, and someone throwing a football through a tire hanging from a rope.

I didn't know quite how to put it. I certainly didn't know how to say any of the words in Hindi. "It makes your dick hard" is *not* something they teach you on Rosetta Stone. But through some rudimentary hand gestures and help from Deepesh, we got it sorted out. The guys couldn't believe it.

"Sir, in America they have pill for everything," Rinku marveled.

I told him that I thought he had a pretty good grasp of the American pharmaceutical market.

TOP: MLB relief pitcher Brian Wilson in Shivaji Park in Mumbai on November 18, 2007, with would-be contestants the day before the kickoff of *Million Dollar Arm*

LEFT: Dinesh Kumar Patel, Vaibhav Bassi, and Rinku Singh in Delhi

The handsome gang of *Million Dollar Arm*'s finals in March 2008

TOP: Rinku wins the finals and India's first Gatorade bath

RIGHT: Ambassador David C. Mulford throws some pitches with Rinku, Dinesh, and their translator, Deepesh Solanki, in Delhi right before they left for the United States

Dinesh, Deepesh, and Rinku in their licensed merchandise gear from my closet in front of our house in LA

Doing drills with
Coach Tom House

Just part of the team: in the
dugout during a practice with
USC's baseball players

Rinku throwing batting
practice at USC

"Mr. Perfect Pitching
Mechanics" Dinesh
displaying good
form at USC

Randy Johnson paying the guys and Coach House a visit at Dedeaux Field

Dinesh, Barry Bonds, and Rinku at a D.C. United soccer game

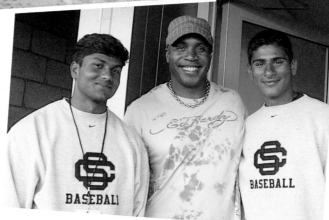

Rinku pitching for the Pirates against the Yankees in the minors (July 4, 2009)

Dinesh in his Pirates uniform at the kickoff for season two of *The Million Dollar Arm* in Delhi in 2011

A heroes' return to Dinesh's village of Khanpur on October 31, 2008

President Obama gives Dinesh his seal of approval at the White House on May 24, 2010

On set at USC, August 2013. From left to right: Pitobash Tripathy (actor playing Deep), producer Gordon Gray, Madhur Mittal (actor playing Dinesh), Jon Hamm (me!), director Craig Gillespie, producer Mark Ciardi, me, Suraj Sharma (actor playing Rinku), and producer Kevin Halloran

On set in Atlanta, May 2013. From left to right: Aasif Mandvi (actor playing Ash), me, Mark, Madhur, Jon, Rinku, and Suraj

Fake Ash and Real Ash

Dinesh, Lisa LaFon, and Rinku at dinner during the movie shoot in Atlanta

Will Chang, me, Jon, and Ash on set in Mumbai in May 2013

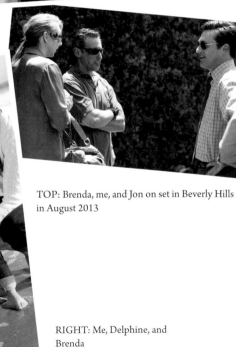

TOP: Brenda, me, and Jon on set in Beverly Hills in August 2013

RIGHT: Me, Delphine, and Brenda

My two sons . .

Dinesh, Rinku, and Deepesh get some wisdom from Korea's first MLB player, Chan Ho Park

Rinku, Will Chang, and Dinesh at the Beverly Wilshire in Los Angeles, CA, January 2008

*　*　*

Since coming to the United States, it seemed like everything they did was something they were doing for the first time.

When we went to the movies to see *Iron Man*—in 3-D, no less—Dinesh and Rinku swore they had never been to a real movie theater like this before and had seen most of the Bollywood films they knew on TV. They did an impression of a movie projector making clicking noises to imitate the closest thing to a theater they had encountered. Armed with fountain drinks and a bag of popcorn as big as a paper grocery bag, we took our seats in the huge amphitheater just as the lights were going down.

"Okay, guys, put the glasses on," I said. "The movie is starting."

"Sir, we have good eyes," Dinesh said.

There was no way to explain it.

"Just shut up, put the glasses on, and watch."

After the movie started up, they were frozen in their seats. When gunfire exploded on the screen, I swear Dinesh thought he was hit. When Iron Man got in a dogfight with a couple of fighter jets, I thought Rinku was going to run for cover.

Afterward, they were sweaty, excited, sugar- and sodium-crazed messes, but they loved every minute.

"Sir, can we see it again?" Rinku asked.

When I told them that the tickets cost $18 a pop (the average price of a movie ticket in India is $2), they couldn't believe it and then quietly dropped their 3-D glasses in the deposit bin.

Baseball was the priority, but on weekends, I tried to expose them to everything I could. When I learned that neither of them had ever seen the ocean in real life before, I took them straight to Venice Beach.

At first, the two of them just stared at the white-capped waves churning in front of the never-ending dark waters. Finally, without speaking, they got up enough nerve to roll up their pant legs and wade in up to their calves. Not a second later, they came running back to where I sat on the sand. Both wore the same expression, a charged mix of exhilaration and terror.

"Sir!" Rinku shouted. "Something is grabbing to our feet!"

What they had felt was the powerful undertow of the Pacific Ocean, something strange and hidden below the surface, rushing to pull them out to somewhere terrifying and unknown.

CHAPTER 6

The members of the Trojans, USC's baseball team, were suiting up. Clean white-and-maroon uniforms hung neatly from solid-wood lockers in the bright, carpeted locker room.

Dinesh and Rinku looked at the baseball shirts and pants with trepidation. They had never put on a real baseball uniform before, since the ones I'd ordered for *Million Dollar Arm* were basically the sports equivalent of one of those T-shirts with a picture of a tuxedo on the front. While the rest of the locker room was buzzing with the energy of young athletes ready to hit the field, Rinku and Dinesh moved with the trepidation of those completely out of their element.

Suddenly Deepesh yelled from the other side of the locker room, "Coach, sir! Small problem . . . Dinesh's cup too big."

The previously boisterous locker room came to a screeching halt.

"Dinesh need smaller cup!"

The locker room erupted in laughter while Dinesh and Deepesh looked around with expressions of utter confusion. To find out what the hell was going on, I pushed through the USC guys and back to where Dinesh stood.

If there was a section in *Baseball for Dummies* that covered athletic supporters and their societal implications, they clearly hadn't read that far. Cups are measured by height and weight, not the size of a man's penis. But manhood is manhood. The cup that Dinesh had been given was for a taller guy and dug into where his groin met his thigh. He had told Deepesh, who translated a little too literally. Shouted across the locker room, it came off crazy. There was nothing to do but grab a better-fitting cup, shake off the episode, and get out on the field.

If they weren't intimidated by a roomful of NCAA athletes laughing at the inadvertent small-penis joke, then the perfectly manicured natural grass of Dedeaux Field did the trick. With 2,500 seats, stadium lighting, and real dugouts, the Trojans' home field was a lot nicer than most professional cricket fields in India. Rinku and Dinesh fidgeted with their baseball caps, which, like everything else, felt new and strange.

Well, even if they were nervous going into that first day of training with the USC baseball team, I was only optimistic. I had been telling the team's pitching coach, Tom House, that Rinku and Dinesh were going to make him look like a genius. And if anyone could make Rinku and Dinesh look like pitchers, it was Tom.

Part of the reason I had brought Dinesh and Rinku to USC was the college's world-class training facility, where everything—the weight room, the dieticians, the trainers, the equipment, the field, and the batters—was not only the best but also all under one roof. However, the real draw was Coach House.

Ray Poitevint had been the one to suggest that Dinesh and Rinku work with Tom, who was well known throughout baseball as a pitching guru who had worked with everyone from Randy Johnson, to Greg Maddux, to Kerry Wood. When Nolan Ryan, author of a record seven no-hitters and winner of 324 games, was inducted into the Hall of Fame in 1999, he acknowledged the profound influence Tom's coaching had on his career when both were with the Texas Rangers in the mid-1980s.

Before becoming a coach, Tom had been a journeyman major-league relief pitcher for eight years. He had some good seasons along the way, like 1974, when he came out of the bullpen to go 6-2 with 11 saves and a 1.93 earned run average for the Atlanta Braves. There's a picture of Tom in the Baseball Hall of Fame, but only because he happened to be standing in the Braves' bullpen when his teammate Hank Aaron hit his 715th career home run on April 8, 1974, breaking Babe Ruth's all-time record. The twenty-six-year-old lefty caught the historic ball on a fly, and the photo immortalized Tom as he ran onto the field and presented it to the new home run champ.

Tom may have had some limitations as a player, but

as a coach he is unparalleled. After his retirement as a pitcher, he reinvented himself as one of the greatest—and most unorthodox—pitching coaches in the game. He was motivated to break out of the mold, because, in his opinion, conventional baseball wisdom simply didn't work for far too many players. "Baseball is a game of failure coached by negative people in a misinformation environment," he wrote in *The Pitching Edge,* just one of several books he has published on the sport.

To find new and better ways to help pitchers, he invented novel training techniques to deal with old problems. One of the major issues Tom noted had to do with consistency. Most guys simply couldn't master the ability to pitch with the same arm motion and release point by throwing baseballs over and over. After examining throwing in other kinds of sports, he realized that there is only one way to throw a football that will produce a spiral. So he got his players throwing footballs to see if the repetition would transfer, and, sure enough, their baseball pitches became more reliable.

A stocky, blond, soft-spoken throwback, Tom isn't afraid to try new things. To this end, he keeps abreast of all the latest in technology. Unlike many coaches in pro sports, Tom believes the naked eye is deceptive. That's why he films all of his guys in 3-D at a thousand frames per second and then breaks down the footage in super slow motion to get a truly comprehensive understanding of what is happening. He watches it all, wearing his glasses down at the end of his nose.

The 3-D analysis is just one element of Tom's amazing thoroughness. He keeps a binder with an entry for each of his pitchers that logs every aspect of their conditioning, from exercise, to sleep, to diet. He is so well versed in the effects of nutrition that just by looking at Rinku's and Dinesh's fingernails, he could tell what adjustments they needed to make to their diets.

Perhaps the biggest component of Tom's ongoing success with developing pitchers is his belief that 90 percent of failure is in your head. As part of his training in becoming a coach, Tom earned a PhD in sports psychology. Even if he didn't have his doctorate, he's just one of those guys who knows how to read and reach people. Tom is the ultimate attitude guy. He will be the first to say that if you have the natural talent, the only person who can beat you is yourself.

It was for all these reasons—that Tom marched to the beat of his own drummer, broke a pitcher down to the most basic elements to build him up again, and believed in the power of the human spirit—that he was the perfect fit for the *Million Dollar Arm* project.

Most pitching coaches wouldn't have wanted anything to do with Rinku and Dinesh. The risk of failure was too high, and the whole project was too unusual. That's what made the project uniquely appealing to Tom from the start. To take someone who didn't know what a baseball was and turn him into a major-league pitcher—well, that was the challenge of a lifetime.

Because I had no idea what Tom had in store for Rinku and Dinesh on their first day, I didn't know how to prepare them except to say, "Work hard and do whatever Coach House tells you to do."

Unlike Ray, Tom hadn't seen any videos of the guys beforehand. Literally the only things he knew were that Rinku was a lefty and Dinesh was a righty. So first things first, Tom wanted to watch them throw. He started from the most basic place: a game of catch. He had Rinku and Dinesh stand about twenty feet apart and told them through Deepesh to "throw it at fifty percent."

Deepesh nodded, said something in Hindi to the boys, and then Dinesh wound up and whipped the ball as hard as he could at Rinku's solar plexus. Rinku used his mitt as a shield, blocking his chest with the glove so that the ball bounced off of it like a failed bullet.

"What are you doing?" Tom shouted. "Easy!"

Deepesh explained it again. *"Aram se,"* he said. "Calm." *"Adha,"* he said. "Half speed."

"Yes, sir. Yes, sir," Rinku said, right before he whaled the ball at Dinesh with everything he had.

Back and forth they went as if they were mortal ene-
mies trying to kill each other, the ball flying off one guy's
mitt and then him running after it just so that he could
bring it back and launch it right back. What Tom—and
I—discovered was that Rinku and Dinesh literally did not
understand how to throw at half speed. When it came to
baseball, they knew only what we had taught them, which
was how to throw at 90 mph. Note to self: we probably
should have taught everybody how to warm up as well.

That wasn't the only problem. Dinesh and Rinku also
had awful throwing motions. They didn't know where to
stand. They didn't know anything.

As Tom put it bluntly, "They threw like girls."

And Rinku's and Dinesh's pitching skills were light
years ahead of their defense. Unlike Dinesh, at least Rinku
wasn't afraid of being hit by the ball. But they still had
trouble using their mitts and had no idea where to throw
the ball if by some miracle they caught it. Every ball hit
or bunted in their direction was an adventure.

Starting from that first game of catch, Tom was extremely
vigilant about preventing Dinesh and Rinku from hurt-
ing themselves. He didn't worry about them learning to
throw hard as much as he was concerned that they might
injure themselves because they had no idea what they were
doing. But so confident was he in his training techniques
that he guaranteed us, whether or not Rinku and Dinesh

signed pro contracts, neither of them would get injured on his watch. He had the track record to prove it.

Before Coach Tom could really show them how to pitch, the first step was getting their bodies ready for the beating. He had to transition Rinku and Dinesh from track and field to baseball training, which stressed different muscles.

After the miserable game of catch, Tom took the guys inside the clubhouse and administered some test where he pinched the guys' skin in a bunch of different places to measure their muscle tone. Feeling Dinesh's arms, Tom said that Dinesh had smaller triceps than his wife.

"You mean I'm weaker than your wife?" he asked through the interpreter. He was fairly shocked to hear this, since in India there were very few women who would be considered stronger than him.

"Yes."

I knew Rinku and Dinesh had far to go when I brought them to America, but I didn't realize that it included woman arms. I felt my huge reservoir of initial optimism draining out of me.

When the guys were back in the locker room, I had a crisis of conscience. At least for Rinku, in the worst-case scenario, he still had $100,000 in the bank to fall back on. But what about Dinesh? Coming to the United States had been a major gamble. If he tried and failed to become a ballplayer, he might still be able to get a job with the Indian army. But there were no guarantees.

From the start of *Million Dollar Arm,* I constantly reminded them of the ludicrous odds they were up against in trying to make the majors.

"You have never played this sport, and now you're competing against people who've been playing their whole lives," I said. "This is our national pastime. This is *our* cricket. The players you'll be competing against probably played catch with their dads every night, then in Little League, throughout school, and during summer camps. At some point, they probably stood in line all day to meet their favorite player. The people you're competing with have been obsessed with this game since birth. Hell, they probably slept with a baseball in their crib.

"And you've only got six months until you try out to catch up. Even if you happen to be the greatest natural athlete who ever lived, that still might not be enough."

At no point had I sugarcoated their chances in succeeding, and yet at the end of this very long first day, I started to feel like I had duped these guys. They had a chance to be in the army and make something of themselves—and instead I had dragged them to LA for a pipe dream.

Tom tried to console me. "Aw, it's not that bad," he said. "Rinku and Dinesh have a lot to learn. *A lot.* But they are gifted athletes."

Tom reminded me of why I had brought them here in the first place. He was able to see all the things in them that I could and even more that I couldn't. Rinku and Dinesh were in the right place to learn. "If they are willing to work as hard all summer and fall as they did that first day," he said, "then they might have a shot."

Tom had a tough road ahead of him but pledged, "I can work with these guys." The question was, could the other baseball players on the USC team?

*   *   *

After a few weeks of basic training, Dinesh and Rinku took the mound and faced live batters for the first time ever. Tom and I had discussed our concerns about what might happen if a batter smoked a pitch right back through the middle. Rinku and Dinesh, horrible fielders, would be all but defenseless against a line drive.

As it turned out, it wasn't my guys that I needed to worry about. The absolute very first pitch that Dinesh threw caught some poor USC student right in the rib cage.

The guy instantly doubled over and fell to his knees. Dinesh might have had terrible form, but he had a lot of strength. He dropped his mitt and ran over to the batter lying in the dirt.

"Sorry, sorry, sorry," he said, hovering helplessly over the batter.

The USC student slowly stood up, took a deep breath, and began the process of shaking off the hit. Dinesh, who didn't know what to do with himself, stayed close to the batter.

"It's okay, man," the batter said. He stepped back into the batter's box—probably as much to get away from Dinesh as anything else. He stood gingerly on the balls of his feet, clearly ready to dive out of the way for whatever Dinesh threw next.

The batter was smart. Dinesh's first pitch wasn't a fluke occurrence. He and Rinku hit batters constantly. In the beginning, just about every other pitch was at least an unintentional brushback. Each of the boys was scary to hitters for different reasons. Although Dinesh had a small, compact motion, which meant that fewer things could go wrong, his pitches were *hard*. As for Rinku, his long, lanky limbs made it more difficult for him to synchronize all the different moving parts. The pitches tended to be more of the fat meatball variety, but no one ever had a clue where they were headed.

I felt bad for these poor USC kids forced to face them. They had signed up for college ball, not a weird social experiment. As they walked up to the plate, the best they could hope for was that they got hit only in the thigh instead of the head. Considering the circumstances, they were great sports about the whole thing. Initially, the majority of the USC baseball community looked at Rinku's and Dinesh's baseball careers as basically a publicity stunt.

The boys definitely received a lot of media attention, which was in no way commensurate with their ability as pitchers. During their first few months on the USC campus, CNN sent a camera crew, and *USA Today* printed a major story. Documentarians Neil and Michael Mandt began filming them for a movie after finding Rinku and Dinesh's blog in June 2008 and approaching me. The rest of the time, Deepesh had a camera at the ready to film the guys pitching, eating lunch, getting dressed . . .

Thank God, none of the USC guys sustained permanent injuries from Dinesh or Rinku. I just wish I could say the same about Deepesh, who one evening made the big mistake of agreeing to help the guys practice their curveballs out in our backyard by playing catcher.

Because Tom told them to keep the curve down, they had to mix them up with fastballs, just like in a game situation. Rinku and Dinesh were using hand signs to signal what pitch they were going to throw to Deepesh, armed not with a catcher's mitt but just Dinesh's regular glove. Naturally, they got their wires crossed at some point, and so when Deepesh was expecting Rinku to drop in a curveball, he confronted a fastball in the high 80s—breaking his middle finger.

Deepesh's was the ultimate act of generosity, but so many people extended themselves to Rinku and Dinesh during their time in America. Barry Bonds became part of this camp when he invited us all over to his house to review the footage I had started to amass of Rinku's and Dinesh's training.

The experience of going to Barry's house, a 17,100-square-foot Tuscan villa in the extremely exclusive and secluded gated community of Beverly Park, was overwhelming for the boys, needless to say. The private neighborhood high above the hills boasts mansions worth tens of millions of dollars, which are owned by some of the richest and most famous LA residents, including Eddie Murphy, Denzel Washington, Samuel L. Jackson, Michael Eisner, Sylvester Stallone, and Wayne Gretzky.

When we drove through Barry's massive front gate and around the circular motor court with a water fountain in the middle, Rinku's take on the scene was to ask, "Sir, Barry Bonds living in hotel?"

Standing under the soaring thirty-foot ceilings of the formal entryway, decorated with columns of Venetian plaster and hand-painted trompe l'oeil murals, I couldn't fault the guy for making that mistake.

"No," I said. "This is Barry's house."

"Come on, sir," he said. "This not house."

"This is a house, bro."

Barry welcomed us in and began the boys' tour by taking us down a long hallway where he displayed a lot of his sports memorabilia. Mounted on the walls were the many, many tangible symbols of his success as an athlete. His seven National League Most Valuable Player awards, twelve Silver Sluggers, eight Gold Gloves (for best offensive and defensive player at his position, respectively), and more were illuminated under tasteful spot lighting. Also mounted behind Plexiglas was a wall of uniforms and gear from all of his favorite athletes, including Muhammad Ali's vintage gloves and fight trunks.

From there we walked through a portico that could have been imported from a medieval Italian cloister. It led to Barry's commercial-quality spa and gym. While strolling through the steam sauna and massage rooms, the boys whispered to me, "Sir, we still in Barry Bonds's house?" I replied that we were indeed still in his house.

At some point during the tour, Barry asked, "You guys got a girlfriend?" in a friendly, offhanded way.

Rinku and Dinesh blushed deeply and shook their heads. Theirs was an extremely modest culture. When I had treated them to a massage to work out some of their sore muscles from Tom's training regimen, they insisted on being worked on by male massage therapists. And when I pointed out a pretty girl passing by in the food court, Rinku scolded me, saying, "This is not good, sir."

Even when I took them to get their hair cut at the local Supercuts, they cringed at the fact that the staff was made up exclusively of women.

After passing the hydrotherapy Jacuzzi, Rinku informed Barry that in India thirty-five is usually considered a good age to get married and start a family.

"I didn't say anything about having kids. I asked about girls."

"Oh, sir, no, no, no," he said. "This is not done."

Barry just smiled and shook his head as he escorted us to the gym, with treadmills, flat screens, and weight training machines. There was also a mirrored wall that opened up to reveal more trophies. *A lot more.*

Barry's mansion had all the trimmings you would expect from the home of the world's greatest baseball player. In addition to the twelve-seat indoor theater, there was a "backyard" with a pool, 2,100-square-foot sports court, an olive tree grove, and an outdoor kitchen with a professional-grade pizza oven and a deep fryer—as well as a two-floor guesthouse that's bigger than most people's regular houses.

Standing by the fully stocked outdoor wet bar, Rinku turned to me and insisted, "*Now,* we're in hotel?"

"No," I said. "This is still his house."

"We just left his house."

"Still his house."

The tour ended in Barry's walnut-paneled office with

leather wall upholstery—the perfect vision of a CEO's lair—where his personal chef, Keith, brought a tray of healthy foods such as smoothies, salads, and homemade bread. While the boys loaded up on the delicious, fresh food, Barry popped in one of the DVDs I had brought, and a mirror transformed into a flat-screen TV once he pressed Play.

"Magic television!" Dinesh exclaimed, pointing at the TV.

For the next three hours, Barry went through all their performances, pitch by pitch. Pausing the DVD to point out small details, he told Dinesh and Rinku the many ways to read a batter. The direction a hitter's toe is pointing in, the bend of an elbow, the placement of the knee—these are all tells that give away his plan. Barry explained to Rinku and Dinesh that if they understand the signs, then they can adjust their pitches to combat their opponent.

At the end of his tutorial, Barry caught sight of a batter crowding the plate on Rinku.

"If a batter crowds the plate, that means he's trying to force you to pitch him outside," Barry said. "It also means that he doesn't respect the pitcher."

Barry launched into a little pep talk. "You're the pitcher. That's your plate. You can't let a guy get comfortable. If a guy digs in too much, throw it right at him. If a guy's going to try to take control of the plate, you have to let him know that you're not afraid to hit him. Just throw at him and let him go to first base. Or at least brush the guy back. The next time, he'll back off."

Rinku and Dinesh looked a little fearful at his advice. They were trying *not* to hit batters. Now the world's greatest offensive player was telling them to deliberately send opponents ducking for cover. Was this such a good idea?

Even though they were new to the sport, they were receiving the baseball education of a lifetime and knew that if Barry was telling them something, they ought to listen. Just being in his house was an amazing honor for an aspiring player, but, on top of that, to have him sit for three hours and impart knowledge was like having Ernest Hemingway give notes on a writer's manuscript, or running lines with Robert Redford. There's not a pitcher alive who wouldn't have benefited from hearing Barry's insights into how batters approach hitting. It wasn't just that he's a baseball expert; it's like having an enemy soldier reveal the other side's plan of attack in advance.

*   *   *

If all went according to plan, less than a year after they arrived in America, Rinku and Dinesh would be expected to compete at the same level as a bunch of kids who were drafted by major-league teams. I was hard on them because I wanted them to be prepared for the difficult road ahead of them *if* they made it. There were going to be coaches who focused relentlessly on the negative. If they went out on the field and got three strikeouts but gave up a walk, they weren't going to hear about the strikeouts when they returned to the dugout. Coaches were going to be looking for perfection. When you play pro sports, you don't get a pat on the back for doing something right. That's what they're paying you for.

But maybe I was pushing the boys too hard. Ever since landing in America, Rinku and Dinesh had been barraged by new ideas and new problems on a daily basis. The confusion of having Barry Bonds tell them that they should sometimes aim at their opponents was compounded by the incomprehensible luxury he exposed them to. At other times, though, Rinku and Dinesh were overloaded by the constant bombardment of instruction and frustration—both on the field and off.

Even their language, the basic mode of communication, presented a challenge. Although they had Deepesh for help, he couldn't be with them all the time. They were determined in everything they did—including learning English. But they both found speaking and understanding it an uphill climb. It didn't help that half the guys around them mumbled or spoke in idioms that made absolutely no sense when translated directly. And nobody was stop-

ping practice to explain "smoke 'em" or "dead duck."
Sometimes Rinku, who didn't like living in the murky
zone of misunderstanding, threw his English dictionary
in the garbage out of anger. He always retrieved it, but it
took a couple of hours of cooling off for him to fish it out.

It was a million little things, all the time. Needing to
ask for help to do just the basic things wore on them.
They were frustrated by not knowing what to order in a
restaurant, how to mail a package home, or how to oper-
ate the satellite TV.

Dinesh had the added stress of feeling that he was
being an irresponsible son by chasing this dream in the
United States. Dinesh was always worried about who
would be providing for and helping his parents in his
absence. Rinku had already won enough money on the
TV show to set up his family for life—although it didn't
seem to make anything easier on him during his time in
the States, as far as I could tell. Dinesh had earned about
$5,000 for coming in second on *Million Dollar Arm,* but
his family, thousands of miles away, still had it tough. The
mental burden that he was off in America, playing a game
that no one he knew had ever heard of, while they struggled weighed heavily on him.

I don't know if that was on his mind when Dinesh came
to blows with one of the USC kids. The baseball player
had been goofing on him about all the usual stuff that

makes guys angry, when, out of the blue, Dinesh popped him one. When he and Rinku returned from practice, Rinku said, "Sir, Dinesh getting in fight today."

That was the last thing I expected from either of them, but in that moment, I realized how hard all of this was. It wasn't just a fairy tale, a Cinderella story; these two teenagers were risking massive failure.

"Did you hit him with your pitching hand?" I asked Dinesh.

"No, sir," he replied.

I didn't make a big deal out of it; he had enough on his plate. Shake it off, move on.

Rinku and Dinesh were pretty good at looking out for each other. They were already friends, but if you had put two young Americans in this same situation, training together every day, eating every meal together, and so on, I am not so sure the friendship would have stood up as well. There was always a chance that one of them would become successful in baseball and the other wouldn't. Ultimately, they were competing against each other for one of the very limited number of jobs in organized baseball.

In pro sports, it's very rare for guys to root for one another. There is simply too much money on the line. The cutthroat mentality is so strong that if a teammate does well, it's usually perceived as a threat—even if he plays a different position. That kind of attitude was as foreign to

Rinku and Dinesh as baseball itself. Rather than becoming rivals, they both looked for ways to support each other, sharing tips, congratulating, and consoling each other.

I admired them for that and much more, but being good guys was not going to land them a place in MLB. Their pitching was all over the place, and they continued to struggle. During an outing in mid-July when Rinku managed to hit five batters in one inning, I hit my wall.

No matter what we did—training, diet, mental conditioning—nothing seemed to help. Watching Rinku lope off the mound, I couldn't help but admit my worst fear to myself: after two months I was beginning to think Rinku's and Dinesh's baseball careers were nonstarters. I was officially feeling desperate.

On the ride home from Dedeaux Field, nobody talked. We were all sick of it: they were weary of the work and frustration, and I was tired of the responsibility. I had never even wanted a girlfriend, let alone a family, and now I was saddled with a ready-made Indian one. These two nineteen-year-olds, who were as defenseless here as newborns, were my charge. Yes, I had cooked up this scheme, but I had been thinking only of the sport, not of all the other things surrounding it. This involved too much stuff that I just wasn't good at.

We got a hostile dinner at the USC food court, sitting at a table together. For me, a rare steak from the Korean

BBQ place that I could tell the boys found repugnant, and it had nothing to do with the shoe leather they'd eaten at Denny's; for them, *saag paneer* from the Indian place, which looked equally disgusting to me, like seaweed and cottage cheese that someone had thrown up. Afterward, the boys watched *Rambo* (their favorite), and I went back to work. But when my cell rang and I saw that it was Ash, I screened the call. I didn't feel like taking Will and Ash along for this emotional roller-coaster ride. I wasn't going to lie to them, just evade.

That night, I sat up in my room with ESPN's *SportsCenter* on in the background, calculating how much money I could save Will if I pulled the plug now. I knew it was a negative way of doing business. How could I factor in all the time and energy that had gone into every sweaty, crazy, difficult moment up until this point? But if the try-out for the pros was going to be as terrible as I anticipated, then wouldn't it be better to cut our losses before Rinku and Dinesh were humiliated and Will hemorrhaged more cash? We had successfully pulled off the contest in India. That was something, wasn't it? We had found a couple of guys, brought them over, and gotten them on a training regimen. No one else had done that, had they?

Maybe that was as much as we were going to accomplish with *Million Dollar Arm*. It was a nice try, but maybe that's all it was.

CHAPTER 7

I carried my piece of plywood out of the clubhouse where I'd stashed it and laid it across a bleacher chair. The California sun was strong, even for a September morning. Luckily, I don't burn easily, since I planned to sit out here for most of the day. A bigger problem was the glare on my computer that I set atop the plywood. I shifted the laptop around until I could see the email replies to the messages I had sent out in the middle of the night.

From my outdoor office setup, I saw Dinesh and Rinku warming up, throwing back and forth to each other, nice and easy. For a few months now, I had been working at my makeshift desk as much as I could so that the guys would know I was around.

After Dinesh threw the punch at a USC kid, it was clear that the boys were starting to crack from all the pressure. Coach House gave me a wake-up call. "You aren't supporting them enough," he said. With his gentle but serious tone, he got the point across. "You need to spend more time with Rinku and Dinesh to counteract their homesickness and mental fatigue."

More time together? I felt like I spent every waking moment with these guys. But I knew Tom was really good about diagnosing that kind of stuff. He did have a PhD in sports psychology, after all. Having told the guys they had to do whatever they needed to in order to realize their goals, I couldn't be a hypocrite. I owed it to them, and myself, to be every ounce as committed.

That's when I realized that I needed to be on-site as often as possible—and that meant setting up my agency on the side of Dedeaux Field. Even on days when I could not work from the stands, I would try to swing by the field even if just for an hour. There was power in my bearing witness to their training. All it took was a quick exchange of glances after a particularly bad pitch for their shoulders to lift again and for them to stand straight on the mound. I wanted them to see me there, to know that I was behind them no matter what. They didn't want to let me down even more than they wanted to succeed for themselves.

I didn't need to sit on the sidelines to know how hard Rinku and Dinesh were working. The two of them were the epitome of diligence and perseverance. When they first arrived in America, I gave them a framework in which to think about their training.

"There is a good chance you aren't going to make it into the major leagues," I said. "After all, most guys don't, and that includes all those guys who have been playing ball since birth. You can't control whether or not you make it. You can only control how hard you work *trying* to make it.

"Most of the American kids you are competing against have at least fifteen years of baseball on you," I continued. "You have to use every available moment to try to catch up. Whatever everyone else is doing, you have to do even more. And that's not because you actually *can* catch up. You can't. But you will regret it if you don't try your hardest. If you go back to India and know deep down that there were sacrifices you could have made, extra time you could have spent at the gym, or ways you could have had a stricter diet, then you're going to beat yourself up. These thoughts will haunt you for the rest of your lives.

"You're only nineteen years old. That's a long time to live with that kind of regret."

Rinku and Dinesh took my guilt spiel—like everything else I told them—utterly and completely to heart. But I don't kid myself that it was my speech that spurred their unparalleled work ethic during the next six months; that was something ingrained in them long before they ever threw their first ball for *Million Dollar Arm.* As Tom put it more than once, "These kids are machines."

If Coach told them to be at practice at seven in the morning, they were there at six to make sure they were ready when he arrived. When it was time for the team to run, Dinesh and Rinku set the pace for all the other players. And when the running was done, and the other players had collapsed on the grass, they were still standing, waiting for more. This was a direct inheritance from their parents, who had instilled in the boys a strong sense of responsibility and mental toughness.

They were never too tired to work. They were never late. And they never complained. They were all baseball, all the time. Pitching is about consistently replicating the same motion through muscle memory. The only way to acquire that muscle memory is to force it into place by repeating the motion over and over and over. Rinku and Dinesh understood this and took it to a whole other level. If they learned how to throw a slider in training, they challenged themselves by returning home at night to practice it one hundred times. Their goal was always to return to Coach the next day doing perfectly whatever he had taught them.

The boys had different ways of learning. If Tom showed Dinesh how to throw one kind of fastball, one kind of curve, and one kind of changeup, he would throw those three pitches until his arm fell off. Rinku was more of a trial-and-error type. He wanted to learn every pitch in existence, asking about forkballs and knuckle-curves and exotic stuff like that. He played around with God knows how many different kinds of pitches until finding the three that worked for him.

But there was no doubt about it, both of them worked like dogs. Doing whatever Tom asked them to do, exactly the way he told them to do it, they were committed 1,000 percent. They weren't robots, though. Dinesh and Rinku were humble but smart. They proved their commitment by engaging intellectually in the project before them. Whenever Coach discussed a certain aspect of their game or baseball in general, they were inquisitive, asking questions that showed that they were taking in and analyzing these new concepts, even with their limited English.

There wasn't one single day when those guys didn't do everything in their power to succeed. When Rinku cut one of his fingers with a steak knife (even though he wasn't eating steak), it was deep enough to put him out of commission for a couple of days. Tom thought that taking a few days off to regroup physically was actually a blessing in disguise, but Rinku was pissed about it.

"You know, I once slammed my hand in the car door and had to pitch the next day," Tom told Rinku in an effort to cheer him up.

"How did you pitch?" he asked.

"I pitched like shit. But I *always* pitched like shit."

Nothing, not even a funny story from Coach, could console Rinku, who announced he was boycotting all metal silverware. And he kept true to his word, using only plastic utensils for three months. Nothing was going to keep him and Dinesh from putting everything toward their goal of doing the best they could at the November MLB tryouts.

* * *

Luckily, they didn't have too many inherent distractions. Women, the downfall of a lot of guys in training, weren't on their radar. And, during the time that the boys and I lived together, women weren't on *my* radar, either. My Indian *The Odd Couple* arrangement put a severe crimp in my romantic life. Bringing a girl back to the house where Rinku, Dinesh, and Deepesh were on the couch watching baseball was more than awkward. It was just weird. So, following my unintended vow of chastity in India, I endured another dry spell for the better part of a year in LA.

They didn't so much as stop to ogle the gorgeous female USC students who used the pool we had to walk by every day to get to Dedeaux Field. (Although double their age, *I* may have snuck a peek from time to time.) Not even California girls in string bikinis, tanning around the pool where the swimming and diving teams trained, could turn their heads. Well, Rinku and Dinesh may not have noticed the girls, but at a certain point, the girls noticed them. While they walked past the pool one day, two bathing beauties waved and called out, "Hi, Rinku and Dinesh!"

The guys froze, holding their equipment bags. No one said a word. Finally, the girls started to giggle. So the guys started laughing, too. A few more awkward moments passed before the guys wrapped up the sum total of their flirtation and continued on to practice.

That kind of single-mindedness paid off. By the middle of August, both of the guys had hit 90 miles per hour on the radar gun. But throwing hard isn't always the same thing as pitching well. They still made tons of mistakes. It was very hard for them to both throw hard and also pitch accurately.

There wasn't any magic moment where either Dinesh or Rinku turned the corner. They just executed the same drills over and over and over until muscle memory started to take over. They quizzed themselves on the same rules again and again until the answers started to stick. Slowly but surely, there were fewer surprises and more quality pitches.

In September they started to pitch in a way that hinted at a professional future in the sport. Once they both began to get a handle on controlling their pitches, I was thrilled to discover that both of them were able to get opposing batters out.

There's a funny thing about pitchers at all levels: some guys throw really hard and look unhittable in the bullpen but have trouble putting batters away in game situations. And then there are the other guys who look like they throw nothing but meatballs but still manage to get results. Throwing strikes is the part of pitching that is more of an art than a skill. It's an innate ability you can't really teach. And for a lot of guys, it's the X factor that determines success or failure in their careers. It's like Supreme Court Justice Potter Stewart's famous opinion regarding pornography: it's hard to define, but "I know it when I see it." Pitching is the same way.

From the start, Dinesh had a few advantages over Rinku, including more strength and a simpler pitching motion. (Back at their college, Dinesh had been the better javelin thrower, too.) But of the pair, it was Rinku who showed signs of gaining control over his pitches first, in July, with Dinesh not far behind.

I had been working at my plywood desk, trying to ignore the bad streak that Rinku seemed to be stuck in. Out of my peripheral vision, though, I could see every time he hit a batter. He had nailed something like five batters in a row, testing my acting powers as I tried to pretend like it was no big deal. All of a sudden, there it was: the clean *thwok!* of a curveball hitting smack in the middle of the catcher's mitt for a strike.

Over the summer, the number of batsmen hit had begun to dwindle and were replaced by strikeouts. By September, both boys had their fastballs working, but this beautiful, looping curveball looked to the hitter like it fell off a table. It had been heading high and inside but then broke quickly and hard, dropping right over the plate for a called strike that left the hitter frozen. That was the start of an unfolding of talent that both Rinku and Dinesh experienced like two baby chicks, beginning to crack the shell.

I'm not a scout and don't pretend to be one, so I don't care how hard a guy throws or what kind of action he has on his pitches. The only basis I have for judging pitchers is whether or not he get outs. Finally, we had something tangible to build upon.

Dinesh's and Rinku's mechanics were far from perfect, but they could both get hitters out. They had an innate ability, the art that can't be taught. As they learned to pitch—not only the muscle memory but how to read a batter's intentions in his body language—their natural ability was intensified and amplified.

Others recognized this ability in the boys as well—including star players who came to the USC campus. One of those was pitching great Randy Johnson, one of Tom's guys and a USC grad. At the time, Johnson was forty-five years old and heading into his twenty-second and final season, on the verge of three hundred career victories. Early in his career, the gangly Johnson had great difficulty maintaining correct mechanics consistently and was extremely wild.

He was also a big left-hander like Rinku. I mean six-foot-ten big. He had a lot of good pointers for Rinku, who was six-two at the time. Randy passed along tips on how to use the whole body when pitching to avoid getting injured. "You can't focus too much pressure on just your arm and your shoulder," he advised. "Your legs and core are critical to generating power and speed."

Randy also shared some words of encouragement, reminding both Rinku and Dinesh what I had told them in the beginning, that there are plenty of guys who play baseball for years and don't make it to the majors. "It's not about how long you've played," he said. "What matters is how focused you are and how much heart you have." Well, if it was about heart and focus, there weren't two players anywhere in the country who had more than these two guys.

"But most of all," Randy said, "listen to Coach House." Nobody was going to quibble with that advice.

The other pro player who made a big impression on the boys was another veteran, Chan Ho Park of the Dodgers. At the age of twenty, he had made history in 1994 by becoming the first Korean to play in the major leagues. Similarly, Rinku and Dinesh were trying to become the first players from India. They were impressed to learn that after having led his country to victory at the Asian Games in 1998, the South Korean government waived Chan Ho's mandatory three years of military service—a first for a country that takes its army very seriously. The exemption enabled him to continue pitching for Los Angeles.

Having gone on to play for the Texas Rangers, San Diego Padres, and New York Mets, Chan Ho had many important insights to share on what it meant to be the first person from your country to play in the majors.

There are a lot of advantages to being first. There's more media attention and endorsements. And if you're doing well, you feel like you have an entire country behind you. But there is also a burden, he said. "Your smallest victories look like mountains, but your defeats look like deep valleys. Everything is exaggerated."

It's hard enough for any player when he fails on the field. But as the first Korean or Indian player, there would always be an added layer of pressure (or fifty). When you don't succeed, you can easily feel like you're not only letting yourself down but also an entire nation.

"You represent your country on that ball field in a way no American baseball player does," said Chan Ho, who would retire in 2010 with 124 career wins, the most by any Asian pitcher. "Your teammates might be able to get away with stuff that you never could. And you are going to deal with jealousy—anger that you're getting attention that isn't being driven by your ability to play. But you'll also have more people rooting for you than most of your teammates could ever dream of." It was a unique position that only a handful of other people in the world shared.

Barry Bonds invited us back to hang out at his palatial pad and watch more DVDs of the guys in action. Back in his captain-of-industry-style office, Barry analyzed each batter while Dinesh and I dug into the sandwiches and fruit salad prepared by his chef. But Rinku didn't touch any of the food. He sat on the edge of his leather chair, watching the magic television, clearly anxious about something. Suddenly he looked at Barry and piped up, "Look, sir! This guy crowding plate."

Sure enough, the batter attempted to intimidate Rinku and take away the inside part of the plate so that he would throw outside.

"Sir, look! I brush back," said Rinku, who clearly couldn't wait to show Barry.

On the screen, Rinku came in high and tight, sending the batter diving for the dirt. Barry let loose a big grin.

"That is how you do it, man," he said, pointing to the

batter, who now kept a healthy distance from the plate. "Now where is he standing?"

"Way back, dude." Rinku smiled.

Rinku and Dinesh had become acclimated to much more than just keeping aggressive batters off the plate. Their English had improved enough for Rinku to break it down with Barry. I challenged the guys to learn five English words per day, with the ever-dutiful Deepesh picking out the words for them. But they seemed to glean even more from the movies they watched nearly every night. They enjoyed walking around the house repeating the catchphrases from classic action flicks and Westerns, like "I'll be back" and "Yippee-ki-yay."

In addition to watching movies, the boys began to listen to American music as well. After going through all my mp3s, Rinku settled on hip-hop as his genre of choice. And out of all the rappers, his favorite by far was Eminem. Dinesh continued to listen primarily to Indian music but also developed a taste for country, of all things.

With all this "culture," the boys improved their communication skills to the point that one day when they returned home from practice, Dinesh told me excitedly, "Sir, Rinku saying something to girl today."

"Oh yeah?"

I pictured Rinku's mother murdering me in a village honor killing when her son came home with a USC girl.

Rinku, in his best impression of a cool guy from a Hollywood movie, repeated his line: "How you doing, baby?"

The words were right, but it was clear from his affect that to him what was cool was not that he'd spoken to a girl. It was, rather, that he had spoken a phrase from a movie. It would have been all the same to him if he had said to her, "I'll be back."

*　　*　　*

Music and movies—even Rinku's adventure around the USC pool—were small diversions from the mounting pressure of the November tryouts. That's when pro teams start signing free agents, as they put together their rosters for next year's spring training. As we moved into fall and our rapidly approaching deadline, it was anyone's guess whether or not Dinesh or Rinku had the stuff to become a pro baseball player.

All pro pitchers have days where they pitch great, and days where they get shelled. All along, throwing 90 miles per hour was our benchmark. We needed Rinku and Dinesh to consistently throw strikes in that range for people to take notice and to accept that *Million Dollar Arm* was not a gimmick. But Rinku and Dinesh swung so wildly between the two poles of very good days and very bad ones that I got whiplash.

One week they would be throwing almost in the 90s. Then the next week they'd regress back to the mid-80s from overusing their muscles. Tom explained that Rinku and Dinesh would be even more up and down than other guys because of their lack of experience. That may have been true, but with pretty rare exceptions, the difference between throwing 85 and throwing 90 is the difference between going pro and going home.

The deadline loomed, and whether or not Dinesh and Rinku actually achieved their goal, it was clear that everyone wanted them to succeed. Even the USC Trojans, who had to face their speeding fastballs at the risk of losing a body part, were on their side. I couldn't believe that not a single kid gave Tom any blowback about the threat of getting beaned in the head by one of these foreign nut jobs. Sure, none of them was digging his cleats into the ground when Rinku or Dinesh took the mound. If anything, they were extra light on their feet, but no one refused to take batting practice from them or even so much as complained about it.

As a sort of thank-you and farewell to their teammates, Dinesh and Rinku invited everyone to an Indian-style dinner at our house. The original inspiration came from an Indian company I had done a deal with called Haldiram's, which makes prepackaged Indian meals. After learning of Rinku and Dinesh, the management at Haldiram's became big fans and started shipping food to the house. Dinesh in particular was a huge fan of the company's *rasgulla,* an Indian cottage cheese dumpling dessert that came in thick, sickly sweet syrup, which Haldiram's sent in huge industrial-size cans. He loved the stuff so much that one time I caught him guzzling it straight from the can. I nearly gagged at the sight, but Dinesh said blissfully, "This *rasgulla* is the best."

Rinku and Dinesh were not world-class cooks, but they were pretty good hosts. They heated up a ton of Haldiram's meals and then set up the dishes with the meal box tops next to all the plates, so the guests could see the names of everything they were eating. About thirty people filed into our house, now filled with the pungent smells of a huge Indian feast. In addition to the USC baseball players, Tom House and Barry Bonds were there, as well as some pros who were training with Coach, including Ian Kennedy, then a young right-hander with the Yankees, and Casey Daigle, who'd pitched for the Arizona Diamondbacks. Superscout Ray Poitevint joined us, too. We all made our way down the long line of chicken tikka masala, *saag paneer, biryani* rice, lamb vindaloo, vegetarian meatballs called *malai kofta, aloo gobi* (cauliflower and potatoes in a spicy tomato sauce), dal, and fluffy naan bread.

It was clear that Dinesh and Rinku were thrilled at the opportunity to share their food and culture with everyone who, for the last six months, had shared theirs. They excitedly led their guests over to the table to explain where the various dishes were from in India and which were their personal favorites. I can't say that everyone liked the food. Indian is an acquired taste, particularly for guys whose idea of exotic cuisine is Cool Ranch Doritos, but everyone at least gave it a try. How could they say no to some goopy dark-colored sauce and mystery meat when Rinku and Dinesh had put themselves out there, trying countless new things every day that were, in turn, frustrating, humiliating, hard, and physically painful? What was a little *saag paneer* in the face of all that?

Watching Rinku and Dinesh work the room, I was struck by how well they represented their country—and not just because of one dinner. In addition to attempting to do the impossible by learning a foreign sport well enough to play it professionally in less than a year, not a day went by during their stay in America that they didn't have to explain an aspect of their culture or clear up an incorrect preconceived notion. No matter how many times someone said something dumb, like, "Why aren't you wearing a turban?" or "How come you're eating meat? I thought all Indians are vegetarians?" they never lost their cool. I wanted to clock the umpteenth reporter who asked, "What is your slum like?" But not Rinku and Dinesh. Their deep integrity and confidence allowed for great generosity in the face of silly stereotypes and willful ignorance.

In their own small way, they were really great cultural ambassadors.

As I tucked into my own plate that Dinesh had brought to me, I was reminded of the original impetus behind *Million Dollar Arm*. Sick of working with spoiled young athletes who weren't appreciative of the talent with which they'd been gifted and the unfathomable money and opportunities afforded to them because of it, I went out in search of those who would understand the value of ability, effort, and relationships. While the jury was still out on Rinku's and Dinesh's pro baseball careers, I could not have found two finer young men. On that basis alone, *Million Dollar Arm* was already a success. For the first time in my life, I was proud of someone other than myself, and it felt good.

In the last month before the tryouts, Rinku was consistently hitting 90 on the radar gun and getting the hang of the curve and changeup. Dinesh was right there with him. By now they had developed a healthy rivalry with each other. Never cutthroat, malicious, or counterproductive, their competitiveness was all about pushing each other to continue to improve every day, every hour, every minute they had left before the pro scouts would judge their pitching abilities. It was hard to say which one of the boys was better or whether either was truly a legitimate prospect. But one thing was for sure: it was impossible not to root for them.

With one week left until the tryout, I asked Jeff Borris, a top baseball contract agent, to watch Dinesh and Rinku pitch on the USC field. Because I wasn't certified by the Major League Baseball Players Association to handle playing contracts, we hired Jeff to be Rinku's and Dinesh's contract agent in the event that either of them got signed. Jeff is not only a close friend and really smart guy, but he is also a huge agent who worked his way up from an entry-level position to part owner of the Beverly Hills Sports Council agency. He has represented players such as Barry Bonds, Mike Piazza, and Albert Pujols in their contract negotiations.

Jeff was the one leading the initiative for Rinku's and Dinesh's tryouts, convincing scouts to give them a chance and watch them pitch, so it was important for him to see what kind of talent he was promoting. I wasn't at USC when he showed up, but Jeff called me immediately to give his verdict on their level of talent.

"Oh my God, this is going to be terrible," he said. "They can't pitch!"

"You probably just caught them on a bad day," I reasoned.

"Bad day? Even if what I saw was the very worst day of their lives, their best day can't be *that* good."

CHAPTER 8

Our biggest risk was stage fright.

Rinku and Dinesh had persevered and done the work. They had focused on baseball to the exclusion of everything else and thrown pitches until their arms nearly fell off. They had overcome frustration, humiliation, and exhaustion to turn themselves into pitchers. Really good pitchers.

In the days leading up to the November 5 tryout in Tempe, Rinku and Dinesh had both been consistently throwing strikes at 90 miles per hour. They knew they had enough control and enough speed to get signed. They didn't need luck or divine intervention. All they had to do was to get on a mound, keep their nerve, and show the world what they could do. This perfect, sunny Arizona day was going to be Rinku's and Dinesh's moment—and the validation of *Million Dollar Arm*.

I was expecting a crowd for their tryout, and that's exactly what we got. The attendance of over thirty team scouts was extremely rare, even in the case of a one-in-a-million high school recruit. Everyone involved with the project— including Will, Tom, Ray, and me—made as many phone calls as possible to any team with which we had any relationship. But Jeff was the one primarily responsible for the turnout. Holding the tryout in Tempe had been his brainchild, and as a big baseball agent, he had tons of connections. He had used the full force of his juice to tell scouts that they did not want to miss out on seeing Rinku and Dinesh pitch.

"I don't know if your bosses made you be here," Coach House said as part of his introduction of Rinku and Dinesh to the scouts, "but I'm glad you're here."

Scouts weren't the only ones who had come out to that strip mall in the middle of Tempe. Also present were dozens of sports reporters from all the major newspapers and television and radio stations across the country. As Rinku and Dinesh remained cloistered inside the training facility warming up, so much camera and sound equipment was being set up that it looked like the site of a presidential press conference.

There was a huge curiosity factor. People couldn't help but be interested in seeing if this odd and far-fetched scheme was actually possible. And, on the off chance that Dinesh and Rinku turned out to be elite prospects, no one wanted to be the one team or media outlet that missed out.

Surrounded by nothing but blue skies on the dazzling fall day, I was so confident that everyone present was going to be completely and utterly blown away that I superimposed a fantasy on the scene before me, in which these two new Indian superstars, surrounded by reporters clamoring for a quote, had MLB teams making them offers left and right.

Yes, the air was charged with hope. The tryout was held just one day after Barack Obama was elected president. As the story of Dinesh's and Rinku's tryout went international, in a lot of countries the historic nature of America electing its first African American president was juxtaposed with their attempt to become the first athletes from India to make it in a big-time American sport. As far as I was concerned, that was a great story line.

While I was riding high, I made a conscientious decision to forgo any kind of pep talk. I was an agent, not a coach, and didn't want to say the wrong thing. I also didn't want to put any more pressure than the million tons already on them from the expectant and important crowd waiting outside to watch them throw. But mostly I didn't want to jinx it. I felt Rinku and Dinesh were ready. That was all.

In that moment, everything and everyone was positive— even Jeff. While Rinku and Dinesh had been warming up inside, pitching in the solid 90s, Jeff turned to me in amazement and said, "Who are *these* guys? They can pitch." I was right. Having caught them on a bad day when he came to watch them throw at the USC campus, he marveled at how different and how much better they looked today. With that last, important vote of confidence, it seemed like nothing could stop us.

Except a mound.

A few staff members from the training facility pulled back the tarp that had been covering the mound since we arrived the day before, and Dinesh climbed it to throw the pitches that would decide his entire future.

"Coach, mound no good."

Dinesh's words rang out like an alarm.

The dirt on the mound, sandy and soft, was different from what Dinesh and Rinku were used to at USC. The texture was not atypical of the pitching mounds across the Arizona desert, but the shifting ground was completely unfamiliar when compared to the firm, compact dirt back in LA. The dirt was just one of the problems with the mound. There was also no pitching rubber, a plank that pitchers use to generate power by pushing their back foot off of it when they deliver the ball. Maybe the worst part, though, was the landing area. The area where the lead foot lands as the ball leaves the pitcher's hand was a one-foot ditch. To put it bluntly, the mound was a nightmare.

We had done a walk-through and scouted the grounds of the Tempe training facility a day before the tryouts. Owned by a friend of Jeff's and used by a lot of players rehabbing injuries, the facility looked great. Inside, the state-of-the-art equipment was sparkling clean. Outside, the field was neat and green. We passed the mound, covered with a tarp to protect it from the elements. It never occurred to me to look underneath.

And now it was too late. The mound had not been prepped properly. A recent rain—an unusual occurrence in Arizona—had turned the sandy mound muddy. The guys had no choice but to pitch on it. They already had so many obstacles to overcome in just getting to this point, but we had thrown in a huge stumbling block in the form of a cruddy mound. It was ludicrous. These guys were used to USC's mound, which was as flawless as anything you'd find in a pro ballpark. The drop-off in quality was alarming.

An experienced pitcher might have had half a chance. Most guys who have pitched their whole lives have dealt with some crummy mounds once in a while. Many grow up pitching off cracked concrete in inner cities or poorly maintained fields covered with weeds. Along the way, they get used to dealing with the little and big variations that attend every single mound. They learn how to compensate and adapt; to deliver the ball regardless of the conditions. At this point, though, Rinku and Dinesh only knew USC.

While Dinesh tried to find his footing on the shaky

ground, a million negative thoughts flooded my brain. All these things that weren't a problem two seconds earlier were immediate, pressing, and ultimately overwhelming.

Why did we do this in Arizona? Why didn't I check the mound? How could I have let down the guys like this? How can I fix this? I want to bring the guys back inside to the warm-up area where the mound is good. But there's not enough room inside for all the scouts and reporters.

The entire year flashed as quickly as my thoughts. The dusty parks of India, the contestants hoarding Gatorade and sleeping on the floor, Rinku disobeying his parents to come to the finals of *Million Dollar Arm,* the flight to America, towel drills, *Baseball for Dummies,* chicken fried rice, fastballs, curveballs, low points, high points. Overloaded and increasingly upset, I froze like a hitter taking a called third strike from the Yankees' Mariano Rivera. I lost control of the situation, as if this were my very first event.

As soon as I started breathing again, everyone else was moving full steam ahead, and it was too late again.

The next five minutes—the worst five minutes of my entire life—felt like they took place over six hours.

Dinesh uncorked his first pitch. As if fueled by the energy of a million nerves, it was so high that it caused something to happen that I had never ever seen before: the scouts, the vast majority of whom stood behind home plate, ducked. Watching pitches behind home plate is what scouts do all day, every day, for most of the year, throughout America and many countries across the globe. They are steely, stony men with large guts from eating mama's meatloaf everywhere from Seattle to Santo Domingo. They do *not* duck. But Dinesh's pitch was so high and out of control that, even though there was a net, the scouts threw their arms up as a reflex.

Dinesh threw about fifteen pitches, one worse than the next. He threw mostly fastballs, mixing in a handful of breaking pitches. All were awful.

When a pitcher does a tryout, the catcher isn't supposed to move an inch. The ball should hit his glove like it was drawn to it by an irrevocable force. When Dinesh pitched, the catcher had to dive all over the place. Many times, the ball wound up in the dirt, bouncing away as if this were some game of catch with elementary school kids. No, that's an insult to elementary school kids. The whole thing was just terrible. When he finished, Dinesh was visibly crushed. Head down and shoulders slumped, he refused to make eye contact with me as he shuffled off the mound.

Next up was Rinku, who had all the same issues as Dinesh. His pitches were just as wild; the only difference was that they were slightly slower.

Rinku's and Dinesh's pitches topped out in the mid-

80s. Their release points were all over the place, and so was the ball. All of the fundamentals they had worked on for months went out the window. If not for the netting around the plate, a few throws definitely would have beaned a scout or two in the head.

Afterward, neither Rinku nor Dinesh had any illusions about how he had performed. No one did. Jeff was upset as well. He felt bad for the kids but at the same time was dreading the egg that was surely coming to his face. Unfortunately, that wasn't the end of the tryouts for the guys. They had to face the many members of the media who had turned out to see what they could do. Talking to the press after a bitter disappointment is tough for any athlete, but nothing in Rinku's and Dinesh's lives had prepared them for any of the trials of the spotlight. In an ESPN interview with Mark Schwarz, when asked if they thought they had done enough to get signed, the boys gave a deflated and resounding "No, sir."

When all they wanted to do was to crawl under a rock and die, they had to analyze their much-less-than-stellar performance, as well as answer whether they had ever heard of Jackie Robinson, Willie Mays, or Babe Ruth. The answer to every question was the same: "No, sir." These guys, who had been eating, sleeping, and breathing baseball for the last six months, still appeared by American standards as if they knew almost nothing about it.

More than a few members of the media wanted to riff on *Slumdog Millionaire,* which had just been released to much acclaim. The blockbuster about a kid from Mumbai who wins $1 million on a game show seemed to connect with Rinku's and Dinesh's story in the eyes of the reporters. One of them asked Rinku, "What is your slum like?"

The media in general, but particularly sports media, want to package stories in the most digestible yet exciting narrative possible. The reporters talking to Rinku and Dinesh wanted to dramatize the boys' journey from slum to coming *this close* to the major leagues—only to face having to return to the degradation of the slums. The thrill of victory and the agony of defeat.

While I understood the concept, it was still offensive to me. And I could see from their expressions that it was also upsetting to Rinku and Dinesh. These motivated kids were from good families who worked hard to keep a roof over their heads and food on the table, as well as give their children an education. It wasn't unlike many American families. They lived the same way billions of others do around the world. "Sir, I come from a farm," Dinesh answered. "We never steal or beg."

Both of them were the epitome of grace during the interviews, answering each question politely, even though I could tell their hearts were breaking.

In the end, the story of Rinku's and Dinesh's tryouts

wasn't the poverty of their native villages or their ignorance of Mickey Mantle; it was how lousy they did on the
mound. All in all, I think 128 countries ran a story on that
disastrous day in Tempe—including India—and none of
them had a silver lining. The piece that ran on *SportsCenter*
was characteristic of the coverage: "Quite candidly, for me
as a scout, they just are not ready for professional baseball," Tom Shanks, a scout for the Seattle Mariners, said. I
almost threw up when I saw it.

In trying to get the scouts out to the tryouts, the most
important point I had worked to get across was that
Dinesh and Rinku were not some kind of publicity stunt.
I told teams that both guys were extremely raw, but they
were legitimate prospects with the unique upside of a billion potential followers at home if they were successful.
If developed correctly, either one or both of them could
generate Yao Ming–level revenue, I argued passionately.
In addition, they would open the door for other prospects
in India.

As impassioned as I was in my pitch before the tryouts,
I was equally reticent after them. Word about Rinku's and
Dinesh's poor performances spread through the sports
community like wildfire. It was a total catastrophe, and it
was everywhere. I had to shut off my phone because the
stupid thing wouldn't stop ringing. I didn't want people's

condolences, and I definitely didn't want them reminding me that they had warned me this was the worst idea ever.

I've made my fair share of mistakes, the same as everyone. But when I look back on almost all the bad decisions I've made, the one thing they have in common is that I went against my instincts. I can usually recall with great clarity the moment in the process when I strayed from my gut and visualize precisely all my motivations and thinking that led me astray. Rinku's and Dinesh's tryout, however, was a blur. I had no idea why I let things happen the way they did. The regrets heaped one on top of the other in a staggeringly tall stack. I should have stepped in. I should have made everyone wait a half hour while we fixed the mound. I should have squeezed everyone inside. So what if it ruined the shot for TV? That wasn't what the day was about. It was about Rinku and Dinesh, two kids with a ton of heart who had traveled across the world to work their asses off for a shot at playing pro ball; to do something that no one in the history of their country had even attempted, much less accomplished.

My original instinct was that it was a mistake to hold the tryouts in Arizona. Tempe had been Jeff's idea. I was nervous about taking the guys outside their comfort zone at USC. But Jeff was adamant, because many of the scouts would already be in town for the state's annual Winter

League, where Arizona minor-league teams send their hot talent to compete after the season is over. Every fall, professional free agents, looking for a new contract, flock to the area. Hence the presence of the scouts. If we held the tryout nearby, Jeff was confident that he could deliver a massive turnout of scouts from almost every team, which is exactly what he did.

"If you ask these guys to travel for a long shot like your Indian boys, a lot of them won't show up," Jeff said. "This is what we should do. It's our best chance."

When it comes to business, I always say that I know what I don't know. If I'm the smartest or most informed guy in a room, I have no problem taking the lead and overriding everybody else. But holding baseball tryouts did not fall under my area of expertise. Jeff's points made sense, so I deferred to him.

But in hindsight, I recognized that these guys were special cases. This was their first time pitching in front of a group of strangers. And there was so much on the line. The guys were uneasy enough with the basics of the tryouts. They should have been in their comfort zone. Every detail of their routine was a crucial component. It wasn't just about the mound; it was also about waking up in their own beds, eating their regular breakfast, tying their cleats in front of the same locker. We added extra levels of difficulty for no good reason. I wanted to kill myself for being so stupid.

Jeff discounted the impact of them being out of their element on their pitching. He hadn't spent six months as these guys struggled to figure out how pizza arrived at their door and why you needed to draw your glove hand in tight to your chest as you went through your delivery. Sweet-talking scouts into flying to California, as opposed to driving a few miles to the strip mall in Tempe, meant sticking his neck out perhaps more than Jeff was comfortable doing. He would never have heard the end of the griping if Rinku and Dinesh stunk, which they did that day.

I didn't blame Jeff. Just the opposite: I was grateful to him for sticking his neck out as far as he did. With very little to gain and a ton to lose, he took Dinesh and Rinku on as a personal favor. Even after he cashed in a bunch of favors to get people to that disastrous tryout, he never gave *me* any grief.

It was on me to trust my gut and advocate for Rinku and Dinesh in the way I knew best. There was plenty of interest to draw scouts to LA. *Million Dollar Arm* had an undeniable curiosity factor, particularly for the media. I had gone the path of least resistance. And then in a flash— with the scouts and reporters waiting while Dinesh stood on the bad mound—it was too late. Rinku and Dinesh had done everything that I, Tom, Jeff, and everyone else involved in *Million Dollar Arm* had asked them to do, and they did it to the absolute best of their ability. They had been ready. Their bad tryout was our fault. But mostly it was my fault.

Ultimately, I was the one responsible for these guys. I brought them over to America, lived with them, ate with them, watched movies with them, teased them, got mad at them. I experienced their frustrations, fears, loneliness, triumphs, and satisfactions. I knew where they came from and the possibility of where they could go. Yes, sometimes they drove me up the wall. But, I realized, I would also do anything for them. I was a confirmed bachelor with no interest in a family, but they had become like sons to me.

I was always fiercely passionate about my work as an agent. It was my life. But everything else in my career up to that point had been business. My other clients were already rich and successful when I took them on, so doing right by them was based on calculations of time, compensation, and image enhancement. With Dinesh and Rinku, I was personally invested in their success in a way that couldn't completely be explained by figures. They had entrusted me to take them out of India, putting their military careers in jeopardy to try this crazy experiment. From the start, I said *Million Dollar Arm* was a numbers game, but I hadn't been totally correct. What I felt for

Rinku and Dinesh couldn't be summed up. At this point, it wasn't about me, or my career, or even *Million Dollar Arm*. The two of them deserved another shot, simple as that. It couldn't be the end for those guys.

*   *   *

After the tryout, we rode back to the hotel, where we picked up our bags and then went directly to the airport to return to LA. It was a long, tough, quiet day.

Tom broke the oppressive silence in the car on the way to the airport to tell Dinesh and Rinku a story. Once, while he was a pitcher for the Red Sox, his manager, Don Zimmer, brought him into a game in the bottom of the ninth at Yankee Stadium. As Tom approached the mound, the famously gruff skipper put the ball in his hand and said, "Just don't give up a home run, you son of a bitch."

Before Zimmer could even make it back to the bench, slugging first baseman Chris Chambliss took Tom deep to end the game. During his lonely walk back to the dugout, Zimmer yelled, "What did I just tell you?!"

Rinku and Dinesh both laughed, but that was the last laughter I was to hear for a long while.

When we got back to the mansion, we each went to our own rooms without a word. There wasn't a glimmer of hope on the horizon. Dinesh and Rinku thought their baseball careers were over before they had started. The best they could expect was a one-way ticket back to India where they would be lucky to get another shot at joining the army.

In their minds, they had thrown away the opportunity of a lifetime and would never have another chance to prove themselves. Even worse, their failure would most likely stop the baseball world from taking India seriously again in the future. That was a heavy weight on their shoulders, and one that I couldn't do anything to alleviate. Many agreed with the boys. One major-league team dismissed the tryout as "a failed social experiment."

For six months, I had watched these guys take everything in stride. They never got too high or low with anything. But now Rinku and Dinesh were launched into a full-on deep depression. They hardly ate and talked even less. They wouldn't say a word. They didn't do anything other than sit on the couch or lie on their beds, not watching TV or talking on the phone but simply staring into space. Crushed, they waited to be sent home as if it were a death sentence. They thought that at any minute I was going to tell them, "Here are your tickets. Nice knowing you."

For several days, we all stuck to our corners. What could I say to them? I felt completely responsible but wasn't going to sit there apologizing, so that the three of us devolved into some stupid pity party. I gave them their space while I brainstormed on how I could save this sinking ship.

But, man, could those guys brood. The storm cloud their mood produced over our heads was so threatening that at a certain point I couldn't take another minute of two comatose Indian kids on the couch. If I was ever going to figure out a way to get them another shot at their dream, I had to get them out of the house.

"Look, I've had it," I said. "I have just had it. That's it, guys. Get back to work."

Jarred out of their emotional and physical stupor, they blinked uncomprehendingly, as if to say, *Huh? What's this crazy guy talking about?*

"Get back to USC. We are working to get another tryout. Proceed as if nothing has changed."

Now I had to make that happen. I couldn't promise that, but I would do everything in my power to get a second tryout. Even if I couldn't pull it off, the worst-case scenario would be that they had to return home—which was their expectation at this point anyway. They had nothing to lose by going back to work with Coach House.

"Stop feeling sorry for yourselves and get going."

They were shocked, but I didn't leave them any choice.

"Get the hell out of the house and get back to what you came here to do."

The next day, they were off the couch and back on the mound. Once they were over at Dedeaux Field, they fell into their old routine. Getting back into pitching turned out to be incredibly therapeutic for them. Tom, the master of attitude, went to work on their minds as well as their arms. "Forget about that last tryout," he said. "Erase it from your memory. As far as you are concerned, it never happened. Just do what you do. You are pitchers; you need to pitch."

I knew that I had two players who were markedly better than the ones that appeared before the scouts in Arizona. They needed and deserved a second chance at USC on their home mound. But I was concerned about being able to round up enough scouts. Although a couple of teams had missed the first tryout in Tempe, the media coverage had been so damning and widespread, there wasn't a soul in baseball who didn't know the outcome. Tom, Ray, Jeff, and I spent day and night strategizing. The four of us worked every angle we could. In the end, the curiosity of the few clubs that had missed the first tryout, and Tom's close personal connections with a few general managers, enticed enough people to warrant a second tryout.

A few weeks after we returned from Tempe, I sat down Dinesh and Rinku when they came home from practice to have a talk.

"Guys," I said solemnly, "I have bad news."

They hung their heads like firing squad victims. They were sure I was going to tell them that we were sending them home.

Then I smiled. "You've got a second tryout."

Shocked and confused, they looked at each other for clarification.

"I told you guys that we would get you another shot. We're doing it at USC, on your home turf, on our terms. No travel. No crappy mound. No media circus. Whatever excuses may have existed after the first tryout won't apply this time around. You're going to get one more shot, and you are going to make the most of it. Life rarely offers you a second chance. But there won't be any more after this. It's do-or-die time.

"So don't mess it up."

Rinku and Dinesh jumped up, hugged each other, and then hugged me. As low as they had been before, they were that fired up now. They had received a death row reprieve. But it was just a reprieve. On their futures, the jury was still out.

In the days leading up to the second tryout in November 2008, Rinku kept trying to psych himself up. Every time he looked in a mirror, he would tell himself, "No fear." But just telling yourself not to be afraid doesn't make the fear go away. The guys were up against much more than stage fright. There was the fear of irrevocable failure; the fear of the end of a long road.

I did whatever I could to support Rinku and Dinesh the day of the second tryout. We treated the morning like any other: they meditated while I wrote work emails, we ate breakfast, they grabbed their equipment bags, and we headed over to the campus. It was business as usual as they warmed up. Tom had crafted their week's schedule so that they would be physically peaking for the tryout. With a total of six scouts, the crowd was very small. The Pirates, the Yankees, and the Mariners were represented—and nobody expected much from these Indian boys.

Again Dinesh took the mound first. His expression of seriousness—the look of a man about to kill someone—set the tone as he wound up for his fastball. His lead foot hit the firm landing area, and he released his first pitch. It seemed to hang in the air forever. Then I heard it. The ball thundered into the mitt. The catcher didn't have to move a muscle. I knew in my gut the minute I heard it: *that* was a real pitch. All my sins, all the screw-ups, were knocked out with that sound. I turned to see the number on the gun. Dinesh's throw registered at 91 mph. It was an awesome feeling, unlike any other.

Dinesh continued to kill it. Boom, boom, boom. It was amazing. As bad as he had been in Tempe was as good as he was in LA. Then Rinku did the same. Pop. Pop. Pop. They both kept bringing the heat. Ninety-one . . . ninety-three . . . ninety . . . ninety . . . ninety-one.

That moment, those sounds, the numbers were pure redemption. Every time the ball thumped the heart of the mitt, it wasn't about whether or not Rinku or Dinesh landed a deal. Earlier, I had said to them that whether or not they were signed, they had to give it their all or risk spending the rest of their lives plagued by regret. There's a reason they pay guys $25 million a year to throw a baseball; it's because very few people can do it at the elite level. But if they tried their best, and their best wasn't good enough, then they had no reason to feel any shame. As we wrapped up the second tryout, no one could dispute that they had pitched to their full ability.

We didn't need proof or external validation. Still, it was nice to get the call.

We knew that they had pitched well enough to get signed, but the waiting was still tough. Over the next few days, there were a few nibbles, and ultimately Jeff got a few offers for Rinku or Dinesh, but no team had stepped up to sign them both.

After about a week, Jeff called me in the afternoon to let me know that the Pirates made an offer to take both of them (thanks to Jeff), which was the best of all worlds. No one could imagine splitting up Rinku and Dinesh.

They each got a $10,000 signing bonus, which wasn't bad for a minor-league deal. *Million Dollar Arm* had started because I didn't want to deal with guys who wanted $1 million payoffs handed over in duffel bags, and, indeed, the sweetest deal I ever brought to a client was $10K. It wasn't just the money. To Rinku and Dinesh, and both their families, $10,000 was very significant, but the pride of knowing that they had done something so historic was immeasurable.

I was more than happy; I was proud. They had not only achieved their dream and mine but also made history.

I broke the news to Rinku and Dinesh as they huddled over a tinfoil sheet of freshly baked Tater Tots. They were back to their stoical selves after the wild emotional swings of Tempe, and took the news with a quiet sense of awe. For a few seconds, they were silent, as if in shock, and then they smiled, and we hugged it out again. Having absorbed the reality that they were going to be the first Indians to play professional baseball in America, they both called their parents in India to share the good news.

Then they wanted to see a map, so they could figure out where Pittsburgh was.

CHAPTER 9

"Rinku! Dinesh! Come downstairs!" I shouted. "Come see what Santa brought you!"

Rinku and Dinesh, still half asleep, stumbled slowly down the stairs of the mansion. Over the last few months, I had celebrated Hindu holidays with them after realizing that part of their training was dealing with homesickness. In honor of Diwali, the Festival of Lights and the most important holiday of the year, we lit a clay lamp outside our home to symbolize enlightenment in the face of spiritual darkness. In a show of cultural exchange, I wanted to share Christmas with them, albeit through the much less serious ritual of Santa.

I didn't have a Christmas tree (I was still a single guy, after all), but I did get them gifts. After I handed them out, they unwrapped their packages slowly, careful not to rip the shiny wrapping paper. I had bought each of them nice long-sleeved shirts without any kind of sports logo (for once).

Neither Rinku nor Dinesh had brought a lot of clothes with him from India, and used to a warmer and more humid climate than Southern California, they were always cold. I told them to take whatever they needed from my closet. They went ahead and raided it for sweatshirts, but everything they wore was either licensed apparel from Barry Bonds or Barry Sanders, or from USC.

The shirts I bought them, warm but not hooded or branded, were so that they could step it up a little from their usual.

"Thank you, sir," Dinesh said. "This is very nice shirt."

"Don't thank me. Thank Santa. It's from him."

"J.B., sir, this is from you, sir," Rinku corrected.

I had told the guys all about Santa the night before, but they weren't buying it. They had gone online to fact-check this "very crazy American festival" and decided that it was nearly impossible that any jolly old guy and his band of elves lived in the North Pole.

"You say it is true, sir, but we not believing Santa Claus deliver us shirts in night," Dinesh said.

I gave up on getting them to believe in the magic of Santa and instead served up a big Christmas breakfast spread of bacon, fruit, oatmeal, and, of course, supercakes.

Not much changed about our living situation and routine as they continued training at USC through the winter of 2008–09. After they signed with the Pirates, they did get a taste of minor stardom. They made the cover of a special issue of *Sports Illustrated Kids* and were also featured in the *SI* March Madness issue. Neel Shah, who worked for the *New York Post*'s famed gossip column Page Six, wrote a six-page spread about the boys for the Indian version of *GQ* magazine. Rinku's and Dinesh's families couldn't believe their sons were featured in the same magazine as big Indian movie stars. Dinesh and Rinku couldn't, either. When the issue with Bollywood megastar Ranbir Kapoor on its cover arrived at the house, they thought I had somehow faked their article inside.

No fifteen minutes of fame would be complete without a little scandal. Shortly after they signed their contracts, a blog called *BabeWatch* made Rinku its "babe" of the week. After making an analogy to—what else—*Slumdog Millionaire,* the blog wrote, "With that solid 6'2" build and that face, he's sure to win over his share of admirers (and groupies) in no time."

This wasn't something that Rinku or I knew anything about or approved of. It just turned up one day on my Google news alert, and when Rinku read the entry, he was furious. He misunderstood the content: "One very, very bad thing about the news is that they say I on the 'babe watch.' This is not true. I not watching girls. I only pitching, training, eat, watch baseball and movies, and sleep." He didn't get that it was saying the babes were watching *him.* Dinesh and I had a field day with it. I printed out about a hundred copies of that thing and stuck them up all over the house to drive Rinku crazy. It worked. "Sir, I am not on the *babe watch*!" he seethed.

The guys didn't have much time to bask—or wallow—in their newfound celebrity. By February, they had to report to Bradenton, Florida, for spring training. I accompanied them to the small city of about fifty thousand people, located between Tampa and Sarasota, that is the home of Pirate City, Pittsburgh's spring training facility. The climate is very hot where Dinesh and Rinku grew up. As they quickly discovered, Bradenton is even hotter.

In the room they shared in Pirate City, there were two pictures on the wall of Bill Mazeroski, who won the 1960 World Series for the Pirates with a walk-off home run in the bottom of the ninth of game seven against the mighty New York Yankees. In between them, Rinku and Dinesh mounted a picture of the god Shiva, to whom they prayed every day. (They had no idea who Mazeroski was.)

Up until this point, they had pitched only to college students. But now they were up against a whole new level of competition as the entire Pirates organization, from rookies all the way up to the major-league roster, worked on the conditioning of its athletes.

A lot of baseball players come into camp really out of shape, particularly pitchers, who are often advised not to throw in the off-season. Meanwhile, Rinku and

Dinesh had been working out really hard for the last eight months—so that they could learn how to throw. On the first day of full-squad practice, every single player was lined up on the field for a warm-up run. When the coach yelled, "Run. Go!" Rinku and Dinesh took his words to heart and ran as fast as they could until they were done.

They were in such good shape compared to everyone else that when they arrived at the finish line, they stood there and jogged in place. The next closest player was about ten minutes behind them, gasping for air and about to pass out from heat exhaustion when he finished.

Rinku's and Dinesh's good condition wasn't exactly appreciated by the rest of the team, particularly some veterans who didn't like being upstaged by two insanely inexperienced foreigners.

"Why are you running so fast?" one of them, panting, asked the guys.

"Sir, excuse me," Dinesh said. "We only have one speed."

It was kind of true, but spring training is a cutthroat environment. A combination of sleepaway camp and a grueling job interview, it is not a place you go to have fun. Everyone from fresh-faced sixteen-year-old high school recruits to forty-year-old superstars bunk, eat, and work out together. With this unorthodox mix, there is under- standably a lot of hazing. Grizzled vets order the newbies to get them food in the cafeteria or carry their duffel bags to practice.

Dinesh and Rinku accepted that they were the low men on the totem pole. Humility was never their issue. They had been playing baseball for only several months, which probably seemed absurd and too easy to a lot of the other athletes. And unlike when they were at USC, Rinku and Dinesh were now in direct competition with these players. There were only so many jobs to go around, and the competition was brutal. Throughout spring training, there are a series of cuts where players are not-so-gently notified by a sticker or ticket in their locker that it's time to pack their bags. When a known cut is coming up, players' fuses are shorter than usual. And in such close quarters, it's easy for tempers to flare. That anyone might lose a roster spot because of two clowns who'd won a reality TV show in India—well, it didn't exactly make the guys popular.

But just like they had at USC, Dinesh and Rinku ignored the politics, put their heads down, and went to work. First, they earned everyone's respect because of how hard they trained, and then they won them over with their true enthusiasm. They inspired the other rookies to push themselves and even the most jaded vets to remember the preciousness of this opportunity to play ball. As the years pass and the inevitable politics of any work environment take hold, it's easy to forget that the 110 people in the Pirates organization are some of the luckiest in the world. They get to play baseball outdoors for a living, and many are paid handsomely for it. Rinku and Dinesh reminded everyone of the privilege of just being there.

The two became well liked by everyone, from General Manager Neal Huntington straight down to the receptionist. Trevor Goodby, who runs Pirate City, called them "a dream."

"They are the nicest guys ever," the equipment manager, Pat Hagerty, told me. "If every kid on our team worked as hard as Rinku and Dinesh, we would never lose a game. They never get in trouble."

As I kept tabs on the boys, I was proud to hear how well they were fitting in. Not that I was surprised. They were that moldable clay that any organization would kill for. The Pirates returned the favor and then some by supporting Rinku and Dinesh in immeasurable ways. They helped them to assimilate into the team and shepherded them through the thorny immigration process. But the organization also went beyond the boundaries of baseball and organized school for anyone who wanted to further his education. Rinku and Dinesh took high school classes and visited sick kids in hospitals, which made them feel incredibly valuable.

After a couple of days in Bradenton, it was time for me

to return to LA. It felt kind of funny being alone, but I ignored the big, empty house and psyched myself up to move on and return to normal. No sooner had I put down my bag than I called up some friends to hang out that night. We made a plan to meet up at Skybar, and I thought, *All right. Game on.*

Located in the Mondrian hotel on Hollywood Boulevard, the übercool outdoor bar with the most amazing views—not only of the city but also of the hottest chicks—is the place to be and be seen. Models and starlets stood against the ivy-covered walls or lounged on large ottomans around the illuminated pool while the DJ spun hip-hop records. As my buddies and I took a banquette, it felt like a usual night in the life of the old J.B., which I was more than ready to jump right back into.

Except that I was distracted all night—and not by pretty girls. I wasn't on my game. I chalked it up to having devoted two years to *Million Dollar Arm.* During that time, I had become seriously rusty. Yeah, that was it. Like a pitcher back from the off-season, I just needed to start throwing and get back that muscle memory.

As I went up to a hot blonde and gave her my classic opener, "Hey, I'm J.B., what's your name?" a small voice gnawed at me. *Really, you are still doing this?* But I dismissed it as quickly as it popped into my head, especially when she gave all the right signs.

The night went by the book. We went home together, had some fun, and, later, after she'd drifted off, I went downstairs to watch *SportsCenter*. I don't remember her leaving later that night or even saying good-bye, although I am sure she did.

I never had trouble being by myself before, but suddenly I was aware of all the empty space in the mansion. As the weeks wore on slowly, I couldn't shake a feeling of loss. There were reminders of Rinku and Dinesh everywhere. The bedspreads in their rooms, the DVDs of movies they had watched a hundred times, and the Bisquick mix in the cupboard all brought up memories. Even sitting on the stupid couch, which had three permanent butt prints from the spots that we always took while watching TV, made me sad. I couldn't believe it: I missed those guys.

It seemed like every little thing in that house made me wonder what Rinku and Dinesh were doing at that very moment in Florida. What movies were they watching? Did they master any new pitches? I kept tabs on them from California. Their life off the field in Bradenton was uneventful. The guys didn't have a car, so they rarely left the training facility. Every couple of weeks, they took a trip to Wal-Mart, and once they went fishing. Dinesh caught a catfish.

Meanwhile, I retreated back into work. I read contracts,

wrote emails, and made calls through lunch and into the evening, ordering in whatever for dinner, and kept at it until I passed out for a couple hours—only to wake up, jump up, and start it all again the next day. I was pounding for my clients, booking as many appearances as I could so that I could be on the road. I also worked my contacts in India as I started to get the ball rolling on a second *Million Dollar Arm* contest.

I was less successful in getting back into the swing of the single life. What I had chalked up to rustiness that first night out on the town turned out to be some kind of permanent injury. I couldn't seem to get excited about anything or anyone. I knew I couldn't work *all* the time, but I wasn't sure what else to do. The bar scene wasn't happening for me, so I decided to call a girl in Texas whom I used to fly in for interstate booty calls on a semiregular basis. Just the right amount of familiar but far away, maybe she was the exact thing I needed to get out of this funk.

As I dialed her number, I thought about one night when the guys and I were sitting around the house watching a movie, and out of nowhere Rinku turned to me to ask, "Sir, why are you not married?

"Sir, you need to get married," he continued, "or soon you will be too old."

Although I was forty and my hair was turning gray, I didn't consider myself too old for anything. But as far as marriage was concerned, I wanted no part of it anyway. Marriage was a scam. My parents had been married for fifty years and my grandparents for seventy, which was great for them, but I never saw that as an example for me, since I wasn't willing to make the necessary sacrifices. I didn't want to share my place with anyone, and I especially didn't want to share my money with anyone. It seemed ridiculous to sign up for something where, if you fell out of love, you had to fork over half your stuff. Plus, most people who wanted to get married also wanted kids. The concept of having children was even more out of my comfort zone than marriage.

Family was extremely important to Dinesh and Rinku. To them, my saying that I wasn't interested in either of those things was like saying I had no interest in food or water. We turned our differences of opinion into a running joke, with them pointing out women everywhere we went as possible bridal candidates for me.

My Texas friend's phone had rung only a few times when I hung up. I finally fessed up to myself that the old J.B.—the one who remained fiercely attached to his freedom at the cost of everything else—was not who I wanted to be. I didn't know *who* I wanted to be, but it wasn't this guy.

* * *

I might have been lost, but at least I knew Rinku and Dinesh weren't, and I took comfort in that. When spring training wrapped, they joined their first baseball team in the Rookie League. The Pittsburgh organization was committed to finding international talent, and the Gulf Coast League Pirates' roster had players from all over the world: the Dominican Republic, South Africa, Colombia, Australia, and more. It was like the United Nations of baseball. For the first time since they arrived in America, Rinku and Dinesh were no longer the only outsiders. With many of their teammates a long way from home, they banded together—unlike a lot of minor-league teams, where it's every man for himself.

During their first season, everything Dinesh and Rinku did on the field made history. On July 4, 2009, in a home game against the Gulf Coast League Yankees, they became the first Indian-born players to play professional baseball in America. Both felt an enormous weight of responsibility when they heard the public address announcer say their names for the first time. Their manager and teammates had put their trust in them, and they didn't want to let them down. They didn't need to worry. Rinku pitched the seventh inning. He threw a wild pitch to one batter, allowing a run to score. But he bounced back to strike out the batter, induce a ground out, and then a pop out to end the threat without further damage. Dinesh pitched a scoreless eighth inning.

On July 13, in the second game of a doubleheader against the Tigers, Rinku became the first Indian to win a pro game in America, although he didn't realize it at the time. Rinku was so focused on getting outs and helping his team, it was only later that someone informed him he'd gotten the win. Dinesh notched his first victory not long after that.

These strikeouts and wins weren't against a bunch of bozos, either. Every player Dinesh and Rinku were competing against was the best high school player in his county, the best player on his college team, or a guy who had been scouted overseas and then brought to America. Everyone they pitched to had been playing baseball religiously for his entire life and excelling that whole time. And now here were two relative novices getting these guys to swing and miss. It was awesome.

For a long time, Rinku and Dinesh had very little sense of whether or not they were actually any good at competitive baseball because of their limited experience with game situations. But once they both got wins under their belts, they realized they were real baseball players. They had done it. Both of them. As I watched them grow into confident athletes and men, I felt a surprising pang of pride—as if I had raised them, which, of course, I hadn't. They had a real home and real families, who loved them very much.

They received the heroes' homecoming they'd earned when in November 2009, after Rinku and Dinesh finished their first season in the minor leagues, I took them both back to India. A year and a half since the end of the contest, this was their first time going home. By this time, Rinku was twenty-one, and Dinesh, twenty.

It was great to see the guys again, although I was quickly reminded of what a handful those two jokers could be. At the airport, I got so mad when I saw how much they brought with them. They had three carts of the most random assortment of stuff I had ever seen. Most of it was due to Rinku's and Dinesh's incredible generosity. They had brought back gifts for everyone (including about a thousand Pirates hats). There were computers and DVDs for their families. But there was also a ton of junk, like old cleats, socks, useless rosters—stuff that most players would have thrown directly in the garbage. When I asked them why they brought it with them, Dinesh said, "Where were we going to leave it?"

"In your locker, like everyone else," I answered before shelling out the $1,000 incurred in extra baggage fees.

I had forgotten that in India you don't just set your stuff someplace and leave, because if you do, it definitely won't be there when you get back. There was a lot I had forgotten about India, including the different speed of time.

Upon our arrival, we got Rinku and Dinesh cell phones, which took hours only to produce the most absurd results. Rinku's phone was what you might call an Indian special. The thing, which must have weighed ten pounds, actually had a pullout antenna and a screen that was perpetually filled with static. It looked like a Sony Watchman TV circa 1980.

On the bumpy ride from the city of Varanasi in the guys' home state of Uttar Pradesh to our first stop of Dinesh's village, Khanpur, I asked him, "Do your parents have anything planned?"

"My brother said some friends maybe will meet us," Dinesh said.

That turned out to be the understatement of the year. As we approached a turnabout about four kilometers from Dinesh's house, we were met by about five hundred screaming friends and villagers. I don't know what I had expected, but the pandemonium exceeded anything the three of us imagined.

The welcoming committee from Dinesh's village loaded us on top of a truck, which, in typical Indian fashion, was twenty people beyond recommended capacity. Then they pelted us with the same colored powders I had been attacked with during the *Holi* festival on the day of the *Million Dollar Arm* finals. At the entrance of the village, a marching band struck up and escorted us in. The caravan grew bigger and bigger as people yelled to inquisitive passersby, "This is Dinesh! He's returning from the United States!" Whoever it was that asked the question dropped what he was doing and joined our gang, so that by the time we reached our destination, the crowd had swelled to over two thousand people. (PS: there are only about 1,500 people in Dinesh's village, so people traveled for this.)

Amid the din of the marching band and cheers, loud even by Indian standards, the procession passed the village elders waiting to place a floral necklace over each of our heads. In return, we touched all of their feet in a sign of respect and said, *"Namaste."* We were adorned with turbans, blessed with prayers, and entertained by a dance put on by a bunch of kids from the local school.

By the time we arrived at Dinesh's uncle's house for dinner, the three of us were officially overwhelmed. His grandmother, uncle, and mother were equally overwhelmed to see Dinesh.

Although his uncle's house was humble, it was clear that Dinesh had been able to make some noticeable improvements to his family's living situation. He proudly showed me the area where they were building an out-house and a cesspool, both of which are rarities in Indian villages.

On a large table outside, Dinesh's mother laid out an enormous feast that she must have spent days preparing. In addition to making Dinesh all his favorite dishes, the family bent over backward to make me feel welcome by driving a ten-mile radius from their village in search of Diet Coke. Thank God, they did find a few cans, because Dinesh's mother made a goat dish that was the spiciest thing I have ever eaten in my entire life. The word "spicy" doesn't even do it justice. My lips, tongue, and even my nose were all on fire for hours. The physical pain was worth it, though, since the dish was one of the best I had in India.

That wasn't the only obstacle I encountered in enjoy-ing my meal. As soon as the sun set, a pack of bats started circling above us, eating the flies buzzing around the food. Every time a bat swooped in to nab one of the flies, I ducked as if Dracula himself were coming for me. Every-one else around the table, calmly eating, looked at me curiously. It was a fitting role reversal from the time I took Rinku and Dinesh to Denny's and presented them with a sacred animal as a snack. Now I was the one freaked out by stuff they found completely normal.

I was able to compose myself for long enough to ask Dinesh's mother and uncle how they felt about his journey over the last year and a half.

"Is it hard for you to understand what Dinesh and Rinku are trying to accomplish?" I asked through a translator.

Dinesh's mom offered a response typical of mothers around the globe: "I am a little concerned because it looks like he is going to hurt his arm from throwing so hard," she said.

"If you could sum up what your wish for Dinesh in life was before the contest, what would it have been and has it changed?" I asked.

After the translation, his mother and uncle vigorously shook their heads no.

"Our wish is always the same," his uncle said, "for Dinesh to be happy and healthy. Even if he is on the other side of the world in America, if he is those things, that is good enough for us."

Similar sentiments were echoed by Rinku's family the next day. We were in their new three-story house, which, by village standards, was as nice as the mansion we'd lived in while in LA. His mom had a bright indoor kitchen. There was indoor plumbing throughout the house, and everybody had his own bedroom. Even though the village was getting only rolling electricity, Rinku's room had an electrical outlet with his own little refrigerator plugged into it. And up on the shelf in his brother's room, I saw Rinku's trophy from *Million Dollar Arm*.

Rinku had first learned about the house a few months earlier during a phone conversation with one of his brothers, who had sent him a photo of the nine-bedroom house. Rinku approved and told his brother that when he got back home, they should think about visiting the house and potentially buying it for their parents.

But his brother was playing a trick. The house in the picture was where the family now lived! They had secretly been building it since Rinku won the money from *Million Dollar Arm*. At that point in the conversation, Rinku found out that his parents had been listening the whole time on speakerphone.

When we arrived at the new house, Rinku choked up. He was not the kind of kid who would ever cry, but the emotions in his expression were pretty close. The money from *Million Dollar Arm* hadn't seemed real to him until that moment when his family poured out of their home to put their arms around him.

Rinku was so happy to be back with his family. He had brought his laptop, and he sat next to his mother, showing her videos of him pitching. His mother had no idea what she was watching. It was almost as if a guy from rural Alabama had landed a lucrative contract playing Quidditch. "I can't believe they are paying you money to throw a ball," she said. Still, Rinku was excited to be able to share his achievements with her.

It was great for me to see the Singhs again, too. I had so much respect for that family. On very limited resources, Rinku's dad and mom raised seven successful kids—two sons are in the military, another used his skill as a runner to land a government job with the railroad, and their daughters married professionals. I sat down with Mr. Singh for a heart-to-heart. As someone who is interested in the ways of successful people, I had to ask him how he did it.

The family had made a commitment to educating their kids, even if it meant that money was tighter than usual, he explained. It wasn't a sacrifice, because they understood their lives as one link in a chain. Their job was to be as strong a link as possible in a chain that stretches back to the beginning of time and forward until the end of time. It's about fulfilling your obligation to both past and future generations. "We just hope our children will honor life," he said.

When Rinku first left for America to become a pitcher, everyone thought he was the village goof. Playing baseball was tantamount to him joining the circus or something even sillier. But his father didn't pay any attention to the village gossip. Yes, his son's adventure was certainly a strange one, but he had faith in what he had instilled in Rinku. "No matter what everyone says, he is my son," he said. "I trust him." The outcome was poetic justice. Thanks to Rinku, his father had a mansion and, rather than delivering vegetables all day every day, paid someone else to do it for him.

Now everyone in Bhadohi, where the Singhs lived, wished for a goof like Rinku. They had as big a procession for our arrival as Dinesh's village did, and they set off fireworks in our honor—or what they called fireworks. Most Americans would probably just call these things bombs. One of them almost blew up a car. The driver got out and started yelling at us, but then some people from the roving mob explained what we were celebrating. And then, just like that, he pulled his car back onto the road and joined the caravan.

At least five hundred kids from Rinku's village came out to greet him. Screaming with delight, they looked up at Rinku towering over them. When he left India, he was probably six foot two and 180 pounds. Not small. But after a year of eating American food, taking supplements, going from 25 grams of protein a week to 300 grams a day, and working out with state-of-the-art equipment, he had morphed into a six-foot-four, 220-pound giant.

While the children nipped at his heels with every step he took, Rinku, who once told me that he'd never had any dreams as a kid, turned to me and said, "Maybe now they have dreams."

CHAPTER 10

When I asked Mr. Singh his secret to family life, it wasn't just academic.

Right before the boys' homecoming trip to India, Rinku and Dinesh stayed with me in Los Angeles for Thanksgiving. But it wasn't just the three of us. There was a fourth—and, no, it wasn't Deepesh.

By then, Brenda and I were officially a couple, the kind that spends holidays together—and if I had my way, a house, a life, maybe even a kid.

In addition to being gorgeous, smart, and successful, Brenda was also a gourmet chef. Literally. Somewhere in between becoming a champion horseback rider and starting a multimillion-dollar company, she also took culinary classes. Instead of making a traditional Thanksgiving meal, however, she wanted the guys to feel at home. So in Dinesh's and Rinku's honor, Brenda prepared an Indian feast from scratch. As she put out about fifteen different dishes—chicken tikka masala, dal *pitha* (wheat-flour dumplings with a dal filling), homemade naan, crispy *paratha* flatbreads, and more—I could tell that the boys approved of both the food and my new companion. But if they thought Brenda was some traditional woman in the mold of the Indian girls they knew (even if she was wearing a sari during our Thanksgiving feast), they were sorely mistaken.

When Rinku needed a ride to get a haircut, Brenda offered to take him in her Porsche. That's when he found out that the woman I was in love with liked to drive very, very fast.

Brenda and I first met in 2010, not long after I moved out of the mansion near USC and into a condo by the beach. Once the guys started their first season with the Pirates, it became abundantly clear that I needed to move out of the big, lonely house we had shared. I chose the airiest, most carefree place I could. That was Marina del Rey. The energy of the city, the tranquility of the ocean, and the luxury of its wealthy inhabitants made it a paradise where I was almost able to forget how lonely I was.

During the Fourth of July holiday, I got a call from my friend Tony Phills, who also works with Barry Bonds, inviting me to a party. While attending a private aviation show, he and Barry had met a woman who was hosting the party on her roof deck in Marina del Rey that she said had the city's best view of the Fourth of July fireworks. I reminded Tony that I also lived in Marina del Rey, and that, with all due respect to this woman, there was no way she had a better view of the marina than I did. Still, I was game.

When Tony told me where to meet him, I thought there was a mistake. "That's my address," I said. It turned out the party was in my building, right across the quadrangle, sixty feet away from where I lived.

I didn't believe in love at first sight or fate or any of that stuff. But meeting Brenda Paauwe-Navori was a serious test of my belief system. From the first moment we spoke to each other, there was palpable chemistry, but more striking were the strange coincidences. Not only did she live in my building, Brenda had also moved to LA from Bradenton, Florida, where Rinku and Dinesh were currently located. If I had believed in fate, it would certainly seem that we were destined to meet.

However, at her party, I was more interested in her long, strawberry-colored hair, full lips, long legs, and kind brown eyes than in destiny, so I asked her out. Over dinner, I got her life story. She grew up in Michigan, the daughter of an entrepreneur and big outdoorsman, who rode horses from an early age. She was accomplished enough in riding to win an American saddlebred (a breed of show horse) world championship. Her impressive accomplishments extended to the professional arena as well. Following in her father's footsteps, Brenda started her own business arranging in-flight services for VIPs traveling privately. She made seven figures a year, drove a Porsche 911, and owned a yacht.

When the economy started taking a downturn in 2008, the private aviation market, like so many other markets, dried up, and she closed her company. In doing so, she paid off every tax she owed, and every employee she had. A lot of people would have declared bankruptcy and left everyone hanging. But that wasn't Brenda's way.

Before Brenda, I had never dated anyone with any substance, and that's how I liked it. My relationships were designed to be disposable. Brenda, however, was what's known as a keeper. It wasn't enough for me to call Brenda my equal; she was far superior. From the day we met, I couldn't get enough of her. I wanted to be around her all the time.

I have a unique gift: if I am headed down the wrong road, I can recognize it. I knew it as an agent when I encountered the young athlete who wanted $1 million in a duffel, and I knew it when sex with strangers was no longer satisfying. My old life was not where I wanted to be anymore, and I knew I had to go in a different direction. I was just lucky that my path crossed with Brenda's and that someone as amazing as her agreed to be with a guy like me.

While I was in India with Rinku and Dinesh, Brenda moved across the quadrangle, out of her apartment and into mine. That Christmas, during a trip to visit her family, I popped the question at a Starbucks in the Gerald R.

Ford International Airport in Grand Rapids, Michigan. The only thing romantic about it was that it was completely spontaneous and utterly from the heart.

"You *are* going to marry me, right?" I asked.

"Yes," she said, right before ordering her skinny latte. That's what I love about Brenda: nothing rattles her.

Although I didn't propose on bended knee with a violin playing and a bottle of champagne chilling at the ready, I fulfilled my obligations with respect to jewelry. In addition to the wedding ring, I also got her a really nice bracelet for the big day of our wedding. As it turned out, Brenda got me a wedding present, too. May 22, 2010, was a big day for more than one reason: that morning, Brenda took a pregnancy test, and it came out positive. Nine months later, our daughter, Delphine, was born.

When Brenda and I were dating, she didn't care that I didn't sleep much. She would go to bed around nine at night and loved that she had the whole bed to herself. It's true what they say about there being a lid for every pot, because Brenda was the only woman who wasn't offended that I didn't want to drift off to sleep in each other's arms.

After Delphine was born, Brenda, who like any good entrepreneur knows how to turn things to her advantage, put my lack of sleep habits to even better use. "I'm getting a breast pump!" she announced. "I'm not getting up in the middle of the night if you are already up." So, like that,

Delphine and I bonded during the middle of the night. When she was a newborn, every two hours, like clockwork, I gave her a bottle. I sat in her room watching her sleep, so that she didn't even have to cry for her milk. As soon as she woke up, I scooped her into my arms and fed her until she was soothed again and back asleep. The guy who swore he would never get married and never have kids now stayed up all night staring at his gorgeous, perfect baby instead of firing off emails (although I got a few of those in, too).

When Rinku and Dinesh came to the United States for the first time in 2008, I got a chance to experience so much through them as though for the first time. A trip in an airplane, the ocean undertow, a heaping Denny's breakfast, a bedroom to oneself in a beautiful house, a fastball landing with a *thwok!* into the mitt after striking out a hitter—all these things and more took on the breath of fresh life. My daughter was an opportunity for all of that and so much more. We taught her sign language so she could communicate as an infant, and my knees literally buckled when at six months the first sign she mastered was "Daddy." With her, I got in on the ground floor of her tasting macaroni and cheese, riding a pony, saying her first words, smiling, being tickled by the ocean's undertow.

* * *

Unfortunately, being close to people isn't all trips to the beach and perfect fastballs. When you get attached, you also share the pain and hurt that is part of every life.

After Rinku's and Dinesh's first year in rookie ball, I got the letters for both boys that the team sends out to agents of international players at the end of the season. These confirm that the athletes have jobs playing a professional sport so that they can get their visas renewed. But after their second year, I received a letter only for Rinku. It didn't take a genius to put two and two together.

At the end of Dinesh's second season, the Pirates let him go. He pitched well with the opportunities he was given. In his first year, he had an outstanding 1.42 ERA and finished with a 1-0 record in 6.1 innings. His second season, unfortunately, didn't go quite as well. Over 9 games, he had an 8.59 ERA and was released by the Pirates in December 2010.

Some might consider him as having a failed career in baseball, but I would trump that argument any day. Very few guys can say they've recorded wins at the pro level, and even fewer perform well enough for a second season. His name is in the record books forever as the first-ever Indian-born pitcher to record a strikeout in professional baseball. He made it to the pros, and he made enough money to change his family's life and become a legend in his village. No one can call that a failure.

Dinesh was able to walk away from pro baseball with his head held high, which he did. It wasn't easy to be let go by the Pirates, but he had the natural gift of perspective that so many others lack. The way he looked at it, bad things happen from time to time, but one has to stay focused on the positive. Dinesh had already experienced way more than he ever imagined when he gave up the $100 javelin contest for the *Million Dollar Arm* finals in Mumbai. He had experienced America, learned how to play baseball, and made a hell of a lot more than $100. The world would be a better place if there were more men like Dinesh.

It's not just about the money. The chance to travel to the United States, to China, to have so many new experiences is certainly a lot more than untold millions of his fellow countrymen, who live in places devoid of opportunity, like Manoj, the sixteen-year-old with a ton of natural talent and the heartbreak of my life. After the finals, I had hoped to get him on the plane with Rinku and Dinesh, but I couldn't make it happen. I was so angry at the bureaucracy standing in his way that I refused to give up.

Finally, a year and a half after the contest, we convinced Major League Baseball International to let Manoj train at a facility it owned in Italy. MLB paid for a first-class plane ticket and agreed to cover all of Manoj's expenses once he got there. It was an amazing deal, way better than what we were offering him with *Million Dollar Arm*. They put the offer in writing, and, as a result, Manoj was finally able to get a passport and a visa. After all the work it took to make it happen combined with the initial disappointment that Manoj felt about being left behind, I was on top of the world with this resolution.

But when Manoj showed up for his flight, the ticketing agent took one look at him, and, seeing a kid from the slums trying to board a plane, figured that something must be wrong. Citing a rule that a passenger needed to have a certain amount of cash to fly to another country, the agent refused to let Manoj, who had less than a dollar's worth of rupees in his pocket, on the plane. Manoj called Ash, who would have been happy to wire whatever money he needed, but it was nighttime in India, and there was no way to get the money there until the next day. So the plane left without him.

The people at MLB International were furious with us. They had jumped through a lot of hoops to get Manoj to Italy and couldn't understand why he had missed his flight. They assumed that he had flaked out and that we were trying to cover for him. The story we told them was inconceivable, and, frankly, I don't blame them for balking. It *is* inconceivable. How could a technicality stand in the way of a young kid's being given a chance to do something special? It was as if the social order couldn't be upended, even for one innocent kid. By this point, Manoj was eighteen. Even if we were able to figure out another way to get him out of the country, realistically, by then it was too late for him to start his training. The end of his story was crushingly sad, awful, and stupid. He never left India.

Dinesh had the presence of mind to know that although his playing career had ended, his life was only beginning. Back in his home village, he could see the fruits of his success. His family renovated their home into a solid-concrete house with six rooms, while Dinesh bought himself a plot of land where he planned to construct another house one day. The money he earned in America also paid for his younger sister's wedding. As he told a reporter back in India, "My family gathered self-esteem and respect in society. It is always good to see your near and dear ones happy."

He returned to school to resume the education he abandoned temporarily for America, but Dinesh didn't completely give up on baseball. He not only taught schoolkids in Delhi the sport but also worked as a pitching instructor for season two of *Million Dollar Arm*. When Ash, Will, and I got the next round of competitions off the ground (which went much smoother than the first; the second time of anything is always easier), Dinesh was a natural—albeit slightly ironic—choice to help train the winner, which he did both in India and at a Major League Baseball training facility in China.

Dinesh wasn't the only one furthering the cause of baseball back in India. Deepesh, his and Rinku's chaperone and translator, was once again working at CKT University in Mumbai. There he put his time in America to good use, coaching the college's baseball team. While Deepesh was in the States, I made good on our promise to get him NCAA certified both as a baseball umpire and a coach, which might make him the only person in India with those qualifications. The whole time Deepesh was in America, he was on a mission to accrue as much baseball knowledge as possible. With the kind of access to coaches and information he was afforded, he wanted to bring back as much wisdom as he was able to cram into his head.

Apparently he was successful in his mission, because the CKT University team was champion for three consecutive years. Not only were they undefeated, but over the course of those three years, not one opponent scored a single run against them. They were like India's answer to the 1927 Yankees.

Rinku, who remained in the States to play in the minor-league Pirates chain, also meant something to baseball in India. At first it took him a while to hit his stride. He finished his first season with a 1-2 record and a 5.84 ERA in 11 games. The fact that he was a lefty, however, worked to his advantage. There are a lot of righty starters, but when it's time to bring in a reliever, coaches usually want to change things up and bring in a lefty. As a result, Rinku got a lot more reps than Dinesh ever did. In his second season, he went 2-0 with a 2.61 ERA in 13 games. Because of his improved performance, he was promoted from the Pirates' Rookie League affiliate to the Class A Short-Season team, the State College (Pennsylvania) Spikes.

In the winter of 2011, Rinku spent over a month working with sixty-nine-year-old Jim Lefebvre, a Dodgers infielder for eight seasons and the 1965 National League Rookie of the Year. He'd also managed the Mariners, Brewers, and the Chicago Cubs. Jim, a close friend of Will Chang's and an early and avid supporter of *Million Dollar Arm,* had generously invited Rinku to stay with his family in Scottsdale, Arizona, while Rinku was trained by Jim and Brent Strom, pitching coach for the Houston Astros. The results were clear: Rinku was in top physical shape and came back with a noticeably improved fastball, curveball, and slider, all of which helped him get to the next level.

Through baseball, Rinku went places that no one, least of all him, could have expected. After his second season, he spent his off-season pitching in Australia for the Canberra Cavalry in the first year of the Australian Baseball League. He also opened the 2011 season in the Dominican Republic, pitching a couple of weeks for the summer league of that baseball-obsessed country. In his second off-season pitching in Australia, Rinku made the All-Star team. His transformation has been remarkable. The guy who used to hit batters left and right is long gone. With impeccable control, he strikes out three or four players for every time he gives up a walk. His off-speed stuff is major league ready, and his fastball can get up into the mid-90s.

The odds are against any minor leaguer making it to the big leagues, but I would not bet against Rinku. He decided along the way that he would do everything in his power to make it to the majors and has been steadily climbing the minor-league ranks. Rinku is not worried about the millions of ways he could get sent home. Instead, he is focused solely on the one chance he has to make it.

I've been around some of the greatest athletes who ever lived, and all of them share the same conviction that life is not worth living if they are not the absolute best at what they do. Barry Bonds lifted weights every day of his life for twenty-five years. Every game day, he watched video of whoever was pitching that night, as well as video of his previous 100 at bats. As soon as the football season ended in 1994, the year that Barry Sanders rushed for over 1,800 yards, he asked NFL Films to give him videotape of every single carry he'd ever had in the NFL. Sometime over the course of that season, Barry had been caught from behind, and he had made up his mind that it was never happening again. Coming off of a season that most would consider unreal, averaging more than 100 yards per game, Barry spent the off-season going through hundreds of hours of tape. He discovered that his "knee lift" and "ankle turn-over" were a little off. And he never did get tackled from behind again.

It remains to be seen whether Rinku has enough talent to become an iconic athlete, but he possesses the same work ethic as any of my top guys. That unique mental makeup is both a blessing and a curse: every second that Rinku is awake, he's trying new training methods and doing whatever he can to push himself further and further.

That drive was in Rinku before he ever stepped foot in the States, but America has changed him—permanently. Just as he no longer throws errant pitches, long gone is the kid who got shaky at the sight of a Denny's Grand Slam. Both his ears are pierced, and he has a huge tribal tattoo across his chest that features his mother's name written in Hindi. He talks like a real American ballplayer ("This is bullshit, man" is a common refrain, making me miss the days of "J.B., sir"), and he likes to fly first class. (Who doesn't?)

But I don't care how much Rinku changes or how hard he pushes himself. He has a good head on his shoulders and is a tremendous representative of his family, his culture, and his nation. For someone whom I pulled out of an Indian village, he carries himself like a media-savvy veteran. When a reporter from India asked him about the decision he made to come to America and the repercussions it had on giving up a shot at representing India in the Olympics by throwing javelin, Rinku didn't miss a beat.

"Sir, I do represent India," he said, explaining how in the minor leagues almost every day he meets people who have never met anyone from India before and might never do so again. He clears up cultural misconceptions and racist stereotypes with kindness and compassion.

"I do represent India by playing baseball in the United States."

And so does Dinesh—a fact that was not lost on Barack Obama. The pair met the president of the United States at a White House event in May 2010 honoring Asian American and Pacific Islander Heritage Month. Naturally, neither Dinesh nor Rinku owned a suit, so someone from the Pirates took them to the outlets near training camp in Florida to buy jackets, shirts, and ties (or "neck ropes" as Rinku and Dinesh called them).

Back home, they were featured on the front page of the *Times of India* in a story with the headline "Two Village Boys Meet President Obama." At the event, they presented their jerseys to the president, which went into his official archive. When President Obama shook hands with them, he encouraged them to "keep up the good work."

I couldn't agree more.

* * *

When I started *Million Dollar Arm,* I thought I was taking a big risk. I worried that I would return from my foray into India having failed to find a single kid who could pitch. It would prove that everyone who thought I was stupid or insane was right. My time abroad would have nothing to show for it other than the neglect of my old clients and the loss of recruiting new ones. I thought the risk in the whole *Million Dollar Arm* enterprise was primarily that of wrecking my career, which at the time was far and away the most important thing in my life.

My partners, Will and Ash, and I were definitely lucky to find Rinku and Dinesh. People in India are like people in all countries; not everyone is a saint. That is particularly true when talking about teenage guys. We could have very easily returned from India with athletes who at best didn't respect the investment we were making in them and at worst got in a ton of trouble.

Despite the radical shift in culture they experienced while trying to learn a sport from scratch, Rinku and Dinesh gave us everything they had—without complaint. It's hard enough for any young man to try to make it in pro baseball, but add to that a language barrier, homesickness, and the pressure of representing an entire country. What those guys achieved was nothing short of remarkable.

But there was never any risk. Not really.

I went to India with the idea of finding baseball talent in an untapped market. What I discovered were the limitless opportunities that arise when you search for potential in those who don't even know they possess it. Looking in unexpected places for the extraordinary expanded my field of vision and changed how I saw the world. In the end, the whole enterprise wasn't so much about finding the best pitchers. It was about giving people a chance to surpass what is expected of them and what they expect of themselves to achieve much, much more.

In witnessing Rinku and Dinesh leave the comfort of home (no matter how modest or isolated it might have seemed to me, it was their whole world) to take a wild leap of faith across the globe toward a goal that made little sense to them, simply because I said they could do it, was nothing short of heroic. I've never had clients who made me less money and yet gave me so much. Whether Rinku makes it to the major league and whatever Dinesh does back in India, they are better for knowing that their lives are what they make of it. And I am better for having been along with them for the journey.

For me, *Million Dollar Arm* was an awakening. In wondering how many kids in those Indian villages could make something of themselves if they had the right advantages, I began to examine what I had made of myself.

Taking inventory, my accomplishments didn't match my resources. I was a hard worker, but even in all my efforts on behalf of my clients, I had kept myself closed off from others. Like Rinku's father said, our job on this earth is to be a link to those who came before us and those who will be here long after we are gone. It wasn't until I helped two guys from India to dream that I had any inkling of what that meant.

In late 2010, after Rinku's second season, he and I celebrated Diwali together at a temple in Mumbai. Rinku read from a sacred Hindi tablet, after which we made offerings of spices, flowers, and money, and then whispered wishes into the ear of a statue of a rat. By then I was a husband with a baby on the way, a description I never thought would apply to me. My prayers during the festival, honoring the inner light that transcends physical being, revolved around the health and well-being of the ones I loved already and the one on the way. For myself, all I hoped was to be a good, strong link for them, as well as anyone else needing a little help to dream.

EPILOGUE

Rinku's and Dinesh's triumphant homecoming became even more of a cause for celebration. While we were still in India, I found out that the *Million Dollar Arm* movie was a done deal.

Ironically, when I originally came up with the contest's concept, Mark Ciardi, the movie's producer, was one in the large group of naysayers who'd warned me that it was going to cost me my shirt and my reputation.

I have known Mark, who had a brief career as a pitcher with the Milwaukee Brewers before becoming a big-time Hollywood producer, for years. Mark is now happily married with kids, but back in the early nineties, when I lived in South Beach, Miami, he used to visit frequently and go with me to clubs to chase girls. I chased the best girl when I was with Mark: my first official "date" with Brenda was at a barbecue at his house.

I know he had my best interests at heart when, in the middle of a Super Bowl event where it was so noisy that the only words he heard me say while I explained my *Million*

Dollar Arm concept were "India" and "reality show," it was enough to convince him I was making a really bad career move.

Unbeknown to Mark, in the summer of 2008, while I was sitting in the USC dugout watching Rinku and Dinesh early in their training, Neil Mandt showed up and told me that he loved the boys' blog and that it could be a great documentary. He asked if he could film as it unfolded and I agreed. He and his brother Michael (Mandt Bros. Productions) filmed their entire training and both try-outs to create a sizzle reel that became the blueprint for the movie. They were pushing it around Hollywood when I called Ciardi and asked him to take a look at it as a favor to me. At the same time someone in his office had mentioned the story, at which point he put two and two together and said, "That's J.B.!"

Yup.

Mark got on board, and suddenly we were making a movie. He brought in Roth Films and Disney, which hired the talented screenwriter Tom McCarthy, who worked up a great script. Not only is Tom a highly respected writer and director, but he was also a writer for and actor in my partner Ash's all-time favorite TV show, *The Wire,* which, from Ash's point of view, was icing on the cake.

From there, the project quickly gained momentum, and after the usual bumps of getting a movie off the page and on the screen, production began. Shooting in India, Mark's experience with the crowded, chaotic country mirrored my own running the contest.

While shooting an exterior street scene in Mumbai, Mark quickly discovered that he was far, far from home. In India, you don't get a permit and then block off a whole area so that the film crew can make sure the director gets the shot exactly how he planned. Normal everyday life continues, whether or not a major Hollywood movie happens to be shooting ten feet away. For this street scene, the director, Craig Gillespie, ordered tons of extras, cows, sidewalk vendors, and more. But Mark shouldn't have bothered. Regular Indian people, cows, sidewalk vendors, and the like randomly wandered into the shot over and over, so that it became impossible to tell who was "acting" and who was just walking down the street.

I was fortunate enough to spend a good amount of time on the set, both in India and back in the States. Whenever I was on the set, my head was on a swivel, since everywhere I went I heard my name repeated.

"J.B. to hair and makeup!"

"Does J.B. wear a turban on top of the elephant?"

"Set up the markers for J.B. on the field."

Most of the time, no one was talking to me; they were talking about the character. They were talking about Jon Hamm.

Meeting Jon, the big-screen J.B., was a unique experience. I'm around big-name athletes all the time, but it's a different story when you meet a celebrity who's agreed to be you in a movie. And there's no bigger compliment in the world than having Jon Hamm play you in a major motion picture.

Jon, a massive baseball fan (St. Louis Cardinals, to be specific), was very loose and funny on set, which, in my limited experience working with athletes on commercial shoots, is always the best way to be. When the star of a movie doesn't take himself too seriously, that trickles down to the lowest rung of the long ladder of production employees. The movie set was very harmonious, and I think that's reflected in the finished product.

Rinku and Dinesh were understandably very excited when they found out there was going to be a film based on *Million Dollar Arm*. When the news was first released, a reporter asked them which actor they wanted to play them in the movie, and they both replied instantly, "Rambo." Not Sylvester Stallone. *Rambo*.

Although their wishes didn't come true, they were good sports, assisting the actors who did play them in the movie to nail accurate portrayals. Rinku was able to spend some time on set with Suraj Sharma (who plays him) and Madhur Mittal (Dinesh) comparing notes on their respective crafts. Rinku talked about getting himself physically and mentally ready to pitch, while Suraj explained how he put himself in the shoes of a guy who was stranded at sea with a tiger for the Academy Award–winning movie *Life of Pi*. Dinesh, meanwhile, taught Suraj and Madhur, neither of whom had ever touched a baseball before, how to pitch.

A lot of the original gang from the *Million Dollar Arm* contest helped to make the movie the best it could be. Deepesh, who worked as a consultant on the film while it was shooting in India, got the opportunity to hang out with big celebrities in his country such as Pitobash, a popular and award-winning film actor who plays him in the movie.

When Tom House sat down with actor Bill Paxton, who plays him in the film, the first thing he said was, "I don't know you from Adam, but my wife says that you're a dude." Tom, who's all baseball all the time, is not much of a movie buff. It is a real tribute to Bill's acting that after only one day together, his portrayal of Tom is virtually perfect.

Naturally, the true story of *Million Dollar Arm* was altered in Tom McCarthy's script. For example, in the movie, the Ash character is married with kids, whereas in reality he's single. (Just saying, ladies!) Also, Ash and I are portrayed as partners in a sports agency that is going under, although in real life, my agency was quite successful, and Will Chang and Ash were business partners with each other before I came along. The movie also portrays *Million Dollar Arm* as my idea with Will as just a financier. Nothing could be further from the truth. Apparently, all three of us had been thinking about the concept of finding another Yao Ming, and when we came together the fuzzy ideas in our head came into focus and took the form of *Million Dollar Arm*. I truly believe that if any of us had not been in the room that day, *Million Dollar Arm* would have never come to be.

But for the most part, it's amazing how faithful the movie is to real life. When it came to sets and props, the attention to detail was mind blowing. The baseball field at Georgia Institute of Technology, where the film was shot, was made over to look like USC's Dedeaux Field, all the way down to the scoreboard. And J.B.'s office in the film is an exact replica of my real office. They took a bunch of photos of me standing next to people like Barry Sanders and Wayne Gretzky, and then Photoshopped Jon Hamm over me.

For the contest scenes, they re-created the original shirts, hats, and pamphlets that we used in real life in all their bootleg glory. The logo used in the movie is the same one created for the contest by Tony, Barry Bonds's creative director and the reason I met Brenda. And a lot of what you see on the screen is the genuine article. Over in India, they borrowed the original pitching cage that we used during tryouts, and all of my original advertising signs and posters.

It was amazing to see how many hoops everyone had to jump through to make Suraj, who is right-handed, play a left-handed pitcher like Rinku. Sometimes Suraj threw the ball with his left hand, and sometimes the director used a left-handed body double. But for other shots, Suraj threw the ball righty, wearing a special uniform that was printed backward in an outfield where all the signs were backward as well. This allowed the editors in postproduction to take those shots and flip them to make him look like a lefty pitcher. In my mind, Rinku's character could have been right-handed, and it would have saved everyone a lot of time without affecting the story all that much. But it just goes to show you the lengths that Mark, Craig, and the rest of the crew were willing to go to in order to make the movie as realistic as possible.

The realism of the movie extends to how the characters interact with one another. The scene where Jon (J.B.) and Pitobash (Deepesh) meet each other is so close to how it really happened, it's scary. Also, the chemistry that Jon developed on-screen with Lake Bell reminds me very much of the way that Brenda and I are in real life.

Even when the movie embellishes the true story, it feels authentic. When Tom first sent me the script, Brenda and I read it separately. After she was finished, Brenda declared that she was mad at me. Referring to the scene where I give her character the same miniature Taj Mahal statuette that I bring back for all my friends back home, Brenda said, "You got those Taj Mahals for *everybody*?" I had to remind her that, not only did I never give her a mini Taj Mahal, I didn't even know her back when *Million Dollar Arm* was first happening in India. The script felt so real that even the made-up parts still felt accurate. I called Tom and said, "This must be the best script ever written, because I just got yelled at for something that never even happened!"

It's a strange experience seeing other people reenact key moments from your life. Watching Jon throw a ball around on set with Suraj and Madhur, who were dressed up like Rinku and Dinesh, was slightly bizarre. But having a major chapter of my life play out on the big screen is a double-edged sword. When I see the way I went about my business in the past, I feel a degree of embarrassment. I'm not entirely proud of everything that I used to do and everything I used to represent. But on the other hand, the movie also reminds me of how much my life has changed.

Not only do I have my own wonderful family with Brenda and Delphine (not to mention Rinku and Dinesh), but *Million Dollar Arm* continues to be a force in India. The contest, now officially partnered with Major League Baseball International, has been renamed Major League

Baseball Million Dollar Arm and is growing in popularity. During the second season, which ran in India in 2010, we had one hundred thousand kids try their hand at pitching, up from thirty thousand contestants for season one. Its third season kicks off in February 2014, and we hope to have at least five hundred thousand kids.

The contest in India is just the tip of the iceberg. We hope over time to add countries such as China, Russia, and South Africa—wherever there are late bloomers and guys who, for whatever reason, have fallen through the cracks, *Million Dollar Arm* will try to be there to catch them. Witnessing firsthand how the kids I met in India made the most of an opportunity when someone was willing to give them a chance is all the inspiration I need to continue the search for talent in places where no one is looking.

I'm thankful that, however long it may have taken me to get my act together, the movie ends faithful to real life, with my character's life headed in the right direction.

ACKNOWLEDGMENTS

Although this book is told from my point of view, it is not only my story . . .

Will Chang, without your vision and partnership, *Million Dollar Arm* would not have been possible. Ash Vasudevan, you were always and continue to be the glue that holds this whole thing together. Deepesh Solanki, your selfless dedication to baseball in India is truly amazing. Tom House, at this point, who can argue the fact that you are the most successful pitching coach on the planet? Vivek Daglur and Vaibhav Bassi, thank you for helping me circumnavigate the unimaginable.

Jen Bergstrom and Jeremie Ruby Strauss at Gallery, thank you for your belief in this book and helping me bring the story to life.

Thanks to Alan Horn, Sean Bailey, Brigham Taylor, Tonia Davis, and everyone else at Disney who fought to turn *Million Dollar Arm* into a movie and then fought again to make it great. Thank you to Jon Hamm, Suraj Sharma, Madhur Mittal, Pitobash Tripathy, Lake Bell, Bill Paxton, Alan Arkin, Aasif Mandvi, Tzi Ma, and the rest of the cast and crew for helping us tell this amazing story and honoring us with your performances. Tom McCarthy, Craig Gillespie, Mark Ciardi, Gordon Gray, Joe Roth, Palak Patel, Neil Mandt, and Michael Mandt understood the potential power of this story when I could understand only the business.

Lisa LaFon, you and I have shared so many milestones in our careers. I can't believe you can still put up with me after so many years.

Tony Phills, I don't know what to thank you more for, introducing me to Brenda or for all the tireless hours you spent helping me make Bonds's and *Million Dollar Arm*'s creative stuff look awesome.

Rebecca Paley, you did such an amazing job on this book. My company and my family can never thank you enough.

Superagent Steve Fisher and APA, amazing job selling this book twice in less than thirty days!

MLB and MLB International, I am indebted to you for helping us continue to grow the contest and bring baseball to India.

Thanks to Ambassador Mulford, Joel Ehrenreich, and the staff at the US embassy in Delhi for all their support.

Mike Tully, for all your hard work on this project, we owe you a great deal of gratitude.

Barry Sanders, Barry Bonds, Emmitt Smith, and Curtis Martin, thanks for believing in me and supporting this dream.

Brenda and Delphine, *Million Dollar Arm* led me to you, and I will do my best to live up to being the man you need.